# Adult Learning in
the Language Classroom

# NEW PERSPECTIVES ON LANGUAGE AND EDUCATION

***Series Editor***: Professor Viv Edwards, *University of Reading, Reading, Great Britain*

Two decades of research and development in language and literacy education have yielded a broad, multidisciplinary focus. Yet education systems face constant economic and technological change, with attendant issues of identity and power, community and culture. This series will feature critical and interpretive, disciplinary and multidisciplinary perspectives on teaching and learning, language and literacy in new times.

Full details of all the books in this series and of all our other publications can be found on http://www.multilingual-matters.com, or by writing to Multilingual Matters, St Nicholas House, 31–34 High Street, Bristol BS1 2AW, UK.

NEW PERSPECTIVES ON LANGUAGE AND EDUCATION: 44

# Adult Learning in the Language Classroom

Stacey Margarita Johnson

**MULTILINGUAL MATTERS**
Bristol • Buffalo • Toronto

**Library of Congress Cataloging in Publication Data**
A catalog record for this book is available from the Library of Congress.
Johnson, Stacey Margarita, author.
Adult Learning in the Language Classroom/Stacey Margarita Johnson.
New Perspectives on Language and Education: 44
Includes bibliographical references and index.
1. English language–Study and teaching–Foreign speakers. 2. Second language acquisition. 3. Adult learning. I. Title.
PE1128.A2J645 2015
428.0071–dc23 2015015293

**British Library Cataloguing in Publication Data**
A catalogue entry for this book is available from the British Library.

ISBN-13: 978-1-78309-416-5 (hbk)
ISBN-13: 978-1-78309-415-8 (pbk)

**Multilingual Matters**
UK: St Nicholas House, 31-34 High Street, Bristol BS1 2AW, UK.
USA: UTP, 2250 Military Road, Tonawanda, NY 14150, USA.
Canada: UTP, 5201 Dufferin Street, North York, Ontario M3H 5T8, Canada.

Website: www.multilingual-matters.com
Twitter: Multi_Ling_Mat
Facebook: https://www.facebook.com/multilingualmatters
Blog: www.channelviewpublications.wordpress.com

Copyright © 2015 Stacey Margarita Johnson.

All rights reserved. No part of this work may be reproduced in any form or by any means without permission in writing from the publisher.

Typeset by Deanta Global Publishing Services Limited.

# Contents

| | |
|---|---|
| Figures | ix |
| Acknowledgements | x |
| Preface | xi |
| **1 Introduction** | **1** |
|     Is Fluency the Goal? | 2 |
|     The Content of Language Study | 4 |
|     This Study | 5 |
|     Organization of the Book | 6 |
|     Methodology | 7 |
|         Data collection | 8 |
|         Treatment of student identities | 9 |
|     My Connection to the Study | 10 |
| **2 Adult Learning Theory** | **12** |
|     The Need for Adult Learning Theory | 12 |
|     Experiential Learning | 13 |
|     Self-Directed Learning | 16 |
|     Transformative Learning | 18 |
|         Meaning perspectives | 18 |
|         Perspective transformation | 20 |
|         Disorienting dilemma | 22 |
|         Critical reflection | 23 |
|         Classroom connections | 24 |

|   |   | The Effects of Adult Learning | 25 |
|---|---|---|---|
|   |   | Conclusion | 27 |
| 3 | Adult Language Education | | 28 |
|   | Foreign Language Teaching Standards | | 28 |
|   | Teaching Methods | | 30 |
|   |   | Adult education philosophies informing approach | 32 |
|   |   | Organization of course content | 34 |
|   |   | Student and teacher roles | 36 |
|   |   | Sources of knowledge about language | 37 |
|   | Moving Toward a New Approach | | 39 |
|   |   | Sociocultural contexts | 39 |
|   |   | Critical pedagogy | 40 |
|   |   | Identity | 41 |
|   |   | Motivation/Investment | 42 |
|   |   | Intercultural competence | 44 |
|   |   | Conclusion | 46 |
| 4 | The Class | | 47 |
|   | The College | | 47 |
|   | The Students | | 48 |
|   |   | The interview participants | 48 |
|   | The Instructors | | 51 |
|   | The Classroom Setting | | 52 |
|   | Teacher/Student Dynamic | | 53 |
|   | Student Performance | | 55 |
|   | The Textbook | | 56 |
|   | Conclusion | | 58 |
| 5 | How the Class was Taught | | 59 |
|   | How Did Students Learn? | | 60 |
|   |   | Direct grammar instruction | 60 |
|   |   | English as primary | 61 |
|   |   | Small-group oral production | 63 |
|   |   | Sidebars | 65 |

|   |   |   |
|---|---|---|
| | Student learning journals | 67 |
| | Film | 69 |
| | Use of Critical Pedagogy | 75 |
| | Conclusion | 76 |
| 6 | What Students Learned | 77 |
| | Content | 78 |
| | Skills | 78 |
| | Personalized or Contextualized Learning | 79 |
| | Learning about Learning | 80 |
| | Learning about Differences | 84 |
| | Learning about Connections | 86 |
| | Learning to Make Sense of Accents | 89 |
| | What Students Did Not Know They Learned | 92 |
| | Conclusion | 94 |
| 7 | Transformation and Development | 95 |
| | Indicators of Perspective Transformation | 95 |
| | Exploring New Sources of Knowledge | 96 |
| |     Evidence from the learning journals | 96 |
| |     Real-world contact | 97 |
| | Becoming More Self-Directed | 100 |
| |     Evidence from learning journals | 100 |
| |     Motivation/Investment | 100 |
| | Critical Self-Assessment | 104 |
| |     Evidence from the learning journals | 105 |
| |     Openness | 106 |
| | Disorienting Dilemmas | 107 |
| | Transformative Classroom Practices | 111 |
| | Conclusion | 112 |
| 8 | Applications | 114 |
| | Summary of Findings | 114 |
| | Implications for Research | 115 |

    Connection to previous studies   115
    Recommendations for future research   116
  Implications for the Classroom   117
    Teaching approach   117
    Learning activity design   117
    Assessment   124
    In short   126
  Implications for Adult Foreign Language Education   127
    The grading problem   127
    The value of language study   128
    Implications for language instructor training   129
 Final Thoughts   130

Appendix   131

References   133

Index   141

# Figures

**Figure 2.1** The experiential learning cycle applied to language learning adapted from Kolb (1984)     16

**Figure 2.2** Learning to Value the 'Other': A Framework of Individual Diversity Development (Chávez et al., 2003)     26

# Acknowledgements

I would like to thank the series editor Viv Edwards for her investment in this book, as well as the commissioning editor, Kim Eggleton. I would also like to thank Cheryl Johnson for her tireless efforts on behalf of this project.

# Preface

Given that most adult language students will not go on to achieve fluency in the second language, L2 study should promote intercultural competence and other kinds of personal development in addition to language development. Adult learning theory explains the ways that adults grow, transform and develop over their lifetimes through both formal and informal learning experiences. This book explores the connections between the fields of foreign/second language teaching and adult learning. This interdisciplinary approach serves as a framework in order to: (a) understand the teaching methods that promote the deeper, more critical sort of language learning advocated by scholars and professional organizations, (b) understand how adult students learn and transform through language study and (c) reinforce the immense value of beginning language courses.

This book details the results of a semester-long case study of one Elementary Spanish (Spanish I) course at the college level. The participants, the instructors and the students are introduced, as is the classroom setting. The hallmarks of this instructor's personal teaching style were direct grammar instruction, L1 use, small-group L2 production, cultural sidebars, student learning journals, a film and the frequent application of critical pedagogy. Student learning fell into seven general categories: content, skills, personalized or contextualized learning, learning about learning, learning about differences, learning about connections and learning to make sense of accents.

Transformative learning theory provided a useful framework for exploring student responses to their learning experiences. Key indicators of perspective transformation were identified in the data; participants explored new sources of knowledge, became more self-directed and critically assessed their own language and culture. These indicators of perspective transformation have clear connections to topics in L2 teaching. Students initiated more real-world contact with the L2, became more motivated or invested and developed higher levels of ethno-relativity consistent with diversity development. Finally, the findings of this study are interpreted in light of current issues in higher education.

Taken as a whole, this book describes the transformative potential of introductory language study for adults and explores how teachers can promote deeper learning in their own classrooms.

# 1 Introduction

As a young adult, I discovered language study and was quickly hooked. The world opened up to me as I gained communicative proficiency and intercultural competence. My obsession with languages led to an undergraduate and graduate degree in language, followed by a career in language teaching at the post-secondary level. For me, learning Spanish as a foreign language was a truly transformative experience; it changed the trajectory of my life. Now, as a language instructor, I see many of my own students undergo the same profound learning that I did. I watch them discover differences, explore connections and take steps into a new culture.

However, unlike me, the college students who take my Elementary Spanish class as a required course in their degree program, or perhaps another professor's Beginning Arabic or German course, are unlikely to go on to become language majors. In fact, they will probably not pursue further language study of any kind after they leave our classes. They will pursue careers in medicine or engineering or education. They will travel to other countries on vacations and meet people from other cultures in their daily lives. But chances are they will not continue to study language in a classroom context. Some of my students admit to me that they do not understand why taking a foreign language class is important at all. They wonder what value it will add to their lives and future careers. I perceive the important learning taking place in my classroom, but many of my students want to know if that learning has any real-world value.

This conversation about the practical value of language study is a part of larger trend. Traditionally, studying foreign languages has been a cornerstone of a liberal arts education and the hallmark of international education. However, around the English-speaking world, there are discussions in the public sphere about the economic and political value of adults learning languages other than English. In a report on the state of language education and policy in Australia, Ingram (2000) wrote:

> It is very significant that the policy seems to see the main justification for fostering language skills as their contribution to economic reform. Despite the value attached to multiculturalism and the maintenance

and teaching of community languages as indicated in the goals, the policy places less emphasis than previously on community languages and most on the economic and international reasons for language teaching.

On a system-wide level, as well as for individual students, stakeholders want language study to produce practical benefits.

These discussions take place amid two conflicting forces: a general cultural push for more proficient speakers in business and government (for examples from news outlets, see Chau, 2014; Chauvot, 2013; Davidson, 2012; Zhou, 2013), and the cutting of programs and funds at all levels (see Lane, 2013; MLA, 2011; MLA, 2012). In the United Kingdom, for example, the importance of language study is widely promoted (The British Council, 2014), yet, in practice, few resources are available to adults who wish to pursue language study (The British Council, 2013). In the United States, many post-secondary students are required to study at least one semester of a foreign language as part of their general education degree requirements and such courses are more popular than ever (Associated Press, 2010), while entire language programs are threatened by widespread budget cuts (Foderaro, 2010; MLA, 2011). World language programs in compulsory schooling enjoy overwhelming public support (Rivers *et al.*, 2013), while the public grants that support such programs are defunded (US Department of Education, 2012).

## Is Fluency the Goal?

The common thread in many of these larger conversations about language study is a focus on linguistic competence, or fluency, as the ultimate goal of language study. It is assumed that in order for language study to be useful, learners must acquire an advanced conversational ability in the target language. Thus, there are many reports on the benefits of bilingualism (see Center for Applied Linguistics, 2010; Fortune, 2012), but fewer on the benefits of limited, short-term language study.

The idea of language as primarily a skill that must be mastered only captures a portion of what happens when adults begin to study a language and culture different from their own:

> Divergent views concerning language and its many functions are reflected in differing approaches to the study of language. At one end, language is considered to be principally instrumental, a skill to use for communicating thought and information. At the opposite end,

language is understood as an essential element of a human being's thought processes, perceptions, and self-expressions; and as such it is considered to be at the core of translingual and transcultural competence. (MLA, 2007)

In addition to the instrumental view of language as a tool for communication, there is also the view that we study language in order to better understand ourselves and others. Through language study, students acquire not only conversational ability, but also the ability to make sense of cultural differences and to understand social interactions across borders.

With the scarcity of resources available for adult foreign language study, our larger public debates about who should study languages other than English (LOTE), in what settings and for how long must be evaluated. Do business and governmental agencies require the skill of advanced fluency from their employees? Or would society's needs best be met if workers had a deeper transcultural competence that allowed positive, productive interactions across languages and cultures?

My intent in this section is not to dissuade anyone from pursuing fluency as a primary goal, but rather to explore why some adult learners feel that fluency is an objective beyond their grasp. While in many countries, foreign language instruction is being expanded at the elementary and secondary levels through traditional language classes and immersion schools (Asia Society, 2014), adult learners rarely have similar opportunities. Even at the college level where it stands to reason that adult students would have the most opportunity to pursue language, few continue on to advanced levels of study (Malone et al., 2005).

The United States government (National Virtual Translation Center, 2007) estimated that in order to attain only a general proficiency in a language linguistically and culturally similar to English, one needs about 600 hours of instruction. On a typical US college schedule of 45 classroom hours per three-credit, semester-long class, 600 hours equals more than 13 semesters of foreign language instruction. To put the numbers in context, 13 semesters is enough language study to qualify as a language major in most American Bachelor's degree programs. Advanced proficiency in a language requires even more classroom hours. In addition, if one studies a language with significant linguistic and cultural differences, such as Hindi or Russian, the number of required hours jumps to 1100, or more than 25 semesters of language instruction, nearly twice the amount of study required for a college degree. A general proficiency in Arabic, which English speakers find very difficult to learn, would require 2200 hours, or more than 50 semesters of instruction, which is more hours than required for an entire Bachelor's degree in the US. It is no wonder, given the challenge of time and effort that gaining proficiency entails, that most US college students, despite taking required language courses as part of their degree program, never become linguistically proficient. In particular, an adult learner taking classes with no intrinsic desire toward fluency would find that commitment especially unrealistic.

In this book, I seek to explore the effects of language study for adult students studying a new language for just one semester. If fluency is not a possible result of short-term language study, then what is its value? This question is of vital importance in recent times as funding for many language programs depends on their perceived value. So, what is the value of taking just one or two LOTE courses as an adult?

## The Content of Language Study

Standards for language learning require a more comprehensive approach (COE, 2014; MLA, 2007; NSFLEP, 2015), one that is broader and more interdisciplinary. Memorizing vocabulary and grammar are not enough. Language instruction should help students 'develop insight into the nature of language and the concept of culture and realize that there are multiple ways of viewing the world' (ACTFL, n.d.: 3) and help 'in gaining understanding and in developing their abilities to think critically about how languages work' (p. 6). Students should learn 'critical language awareness, interpretation and translation, historical and political consciousness, social sensibility, and aesthetic perception' (MLA, 2007: 4).

While these are important goals, the question for many language teachers is how to promote this kind of learning within the confines of a classroom focused on communication. 'Language teachers tend to agree with the notion that what needs to be taught is critical language awareness, interpretive skills, and historical consciousness, but while they find the idea inspiring and exciting, they also find it difficult, if not impossible, to implement' (Byram & Kramsch, 2008: 20).

As a college-level language teacher myself, I can attest that I am inspired by the idea that my classroom can be a place where students discover the world, explore difference and develop their translingual and transcultural competence. Yet, I wonder, how exactly is that done? Are there teachers already doing a good job of developing adult students through language study? Have they left a trail for me to find as they blazed this path? How exactly does an instructor teach for critical consciousness? And finally, to what extent should I make room in my classroom for the development of these skills and attitudes?

Given that linguistic proficiency and other kinds of adult learning all require time to develop, the next issue is one of scarcity of classroom time. That is to say, in order to increase time focused on one kind of learning, must instructional time spent on the other be reduced? The issues for me as a language teacher become: (1) which learning outcomes to promote in my classroom and (2) which methods lead to those outcomes.

## This Study

In this book, I argue that even one semester of language instruction can be invaluable to adult student learning and development. I will discuss the findings of case study research in a first-semester college language classroom. To put it simply, I spent a semester in a classroom paying close attention to what was being taught and how it was being taught. Then, I asked students in the class what they learned, and, while some did report learning language, most discussed learning other things. Students reported learning about themselves, about the act and process of learning and about race, culture and prejudice. They reported changing their perspectives on important issues and becoming more self-directed in their learning. Their stories exemplify the life-changing impact language learning can have on adult students.

The instructor who taught the class I studied for this book was acutely aware that she had no control over the majority of the content of the course because her institution set the curriculum and chose the text. So, she decided to present the required material in a way that spoke to her personally, that reflected her own approach to living and learning as a world citizen. She focused on how to teach instead of on what to teach. This approach is consistent with best practices in many disciplines. To quote my colleague Jonathan Hagood's revision of *the medium is the message*: 'The pedagogy is the content' (2013).

I found that the students in this instructor's classroom experienced profound learning and were usually able to directly connect their learning experiences with her pedagogical choices. None of the students in her classroom intended to major in the language; they all had other academic and professional aspirations that took precedent. Yet, many of her students reported transformational learning experiences while in her classroom and expected to have many opportunities to apply what they had learned outside of the classroom. While I do not hold the instructor in this classroom up as a model teacher in every way (she was human after all), she did one thing very well: promoting adult development through language study. Even if readers disagree with aspects of her pedagogy, I believe we can all learn from her.

Adult learning theory, in any learning context or setting, explains the ways that adults grow, transform and develop over a lifetime through both formal and informal learning experiences. My analysis in this book seeks to find connections between the fields of foreign/second language teaching and adult learning theory. Taking this interdisciplinary approach serves as a framework in order to: (a) understand the teaching methods that promote the deeper, more critical sort of language learning advocated by scholars and professional organizations, (b) understand how adult students learn and transform through language study and (c) reinforce the immense value of beginning language courses.

## Organization of the Book

This book details the results of a semester-long case study of one Elementary Spanish course (Spanish I) at the college level. In Chapters 2 and 3, I examine adult learning theory and its connections to foreign language education. Both of these fields are immense and active with relevant new scholarship popping up seemingly every day. While no book could give a thorough treatment of both fields, there are some key ways that adult learning connects to foreign language education that have practical implications for teaching and learning. Chapter 2 gives a brief overview of some of the major themes of adult learning including transformative learning, experiential learning and self-directed learning. The emphasis is on the processes involved in adult language learning. Chapter 3 contextualizes the foreign language education of adults within a broader framework of best practices, standards and approaches to teaching languages. Here I focus on current and historical trends in how language teachers present content.

In Chapter 4, the reader meets the class at the heart of this study. The classroom selected did not exist in a vacuum. The class was part of a community, a college and a department. The participants, both instructor and students, were unique individuals meeting in one place for a common purpose. I imagine that the class I studied is very much like other adult language classes all over the country. However, the goal of Chapter 4 is to discuss the characteristics unique to this case.

The actual instruction that took place, or rather, the methods used and how those methods were applied, is discussed in Chapter 5. By analyzing the classroom practices and student reactions to those practices,

I demonstrate how best practices in adult language education play out in this particular setting.

Chapter 6 discusses the question of what students learn while studying language. What is taught is not always what is learned. Learning to communicate in the language is often only the beginning of learning for adult students. The learning reported by the participants in this study is profound, multidimensional and not at all limited to the actual language being studied. Chapter 7 continues the analysis of what students learned by exploring language learning as adult learning: transformational and leading to personal development.

Chapter 8 seeks to interpret the findings of this study in the light of current issues in higher education. I discuss ways instructors who teach required courses can implement the instructional practices outlined in the findings of this research. Even those teaching in difficult circumstances, without the power to implement large-scale changes, can apply adult learning theory to their teaching to promote deep learning. I draw conclusions about the value of the learning described by the participants.

## Methodology

In choosing a case for this research, the criteria for my selection were as follows. First, I wanted to study a section of first-semester Spanish at the community college level. I was interested in the community college level in particular because, at that level, language classes are taken as part of the general education core or because of student interest, but not as part of a major course of study. Second, it was important to me to find an instructor with whom I could have a positive, collaborative relationship. The type of research I wanted to do would require me to be visible in the classroom and communicating with the students and instructor frequently. A positive working relationship would be vital. In addition to these two criteria, there was one instructor, Ms Dina Salazar (pseudonym), whom I particularly wanted to observe in the classroom. I had good reason to believe that Ms Salazar was conducting her class in a way that improved outcomes for adult students. During the pilot study to this research (Johnson & Mullins Nelson, 2010), I sampled four sections of Elementary Spanish II to administer a survey and then conduct follow-up interviews. Two of the sections I surveyed were taught by Ms Salazar and two were taught by another instructor. However, all of the participants who exhibited signs of transformative learning came from Ms Salazar's classes. Based both on the high number of students from her classes that reported transformation and on student descriptions of her classroom environment, I came to suspect that Ms Salazar taught her classes in a way that encouraged important kinds of adult learning. Accordingly, I approached Ms Salazar about collaborating with me again.

## Data collection

Case study research in second language education focuses on cultivating a holistic view of teaching and learning and providing detailed descriptions of specific learners or classes. My study had a limited research focus (adult learning) and a pre-determined time constraint (one semester), which McKay (2006) describes as hallmarks of case study L2 research. College calendars are divided into terms, in this case semesters, providing me with a convenient timetable for my research. Following in the ethnographic tradition (Chaudron, 1988; Creswell, 2007), I collected multiple sources of data in the form of participant observation in the classroom (Spradley, 1980), learning/reflective journals from all of the students in the class (Brown, 1985), and in-depth interviews outside of class with the instructor and seven students from the larger class. During the participant observation and interviews, I used audio recording and field notes to record my observations, and then transcribed the interviews based on the recordings. All of the data was analyzed (Coffey & Atkinson, 1996) through the reading, notation, coding and categorizing of my field journal, the student learning journals and the written transcripts from the interviews.

Based on my ongoing analysis of learning journals and on classroom observation, I invited eight students to participate in interviews because they seemed to be experiencing deep learning. The one-on-one interviews were conducted outside of class time using a semi-structured, conversational interview technique. In this less structured, conversational interview style, I permitted my conversations with each participant to be guided in large part by the participant's own interests. My assessment is that a less structured approach allowed me as the interviewer to create a comfortable dialogue with the participants and elicit adequate responses in a way that best fit the particular participant. An important part of this dialogue was that my role of researcher was as important as my role of fellow human being. I spoke with the participants as if I were speaking to my own friends, answering personal questions and giving opinions when asked. I was myself both 'me' the person and 'me' the researcher, and I believe this intimacy and informality created an atmosphere in which participants could speak freely. In a less structured, more intimate interview setting, the participant is more able to open up and delve into personal experiences in her own way and at her own pace (Mackey & Gass, 2005).

Dijkstra et al. (1985) conducted a study in which they compared a formal, structured interview style with a more informal, conversational interview style in which the interviewer maintains no emotional or social distance from the participant. Denzin (1970) proposed that 'the interview situation should approximate maximally routine, everyday social conversation, so that the respondent realizes, "I am in a personal relationship with the interviewer."' Referred to as a 'socio-emotional style', this technique 'is a prerequisite for adequate information reporting, particularly when sensitive, personal topics are involved' (38). Given the deeply personal nature of the subject matter discussed in this research, using a socio-emotional style was deemed vital to the success of the one-on-one interviews.

Another way that my socio-emotional interview style affected the study, in particular this written report of the study, was in my decision not to include tables or charts giving participants' ages, ethnicities and other descriptive information. During the interviews, the students and I discussed their backgrounds and identities extensively. I found out about their complex and changing ideas about race and gender. I heard them describe how their ideas about family and parenting were rooted in their own traditions and were changing as they learned about another culture. In light of these deep discussions, it did not seem appropriate to reduce students' ideas to one or two word responses on a chart. One student, who chose the pseudonym Ten, was of mixed ethnic background and ultimately identified himself as a Black man. Yet, we spent more than 20 minutes discussing his childhood experiences of developing a racial and ethnic identity. Jade had been happily married with three children. Although her husband died two years prior to our interview, she never identified herself as widowed or single. She did discuss that she had been married and was open to dating at some point in the future. How could I reduce these two individual's experiences to 'black' and 'widowed' for my chart? I believe it was the emotional depth of the interviews and the intimate rapport that we developed that allowed me to see beyond simple descriptors for these students. I wanted the written report of my research to reflect that depth and intimacy.

## Treatment of student identities

During the weeks I spent in the classroom, I became increasingly familiar with the students in the class. Because this was an ongoing process,

I was not always able to record the names of students as they interacted in class. Herein, I refer to unknown speakers as 'Student'. By the time I began identifying evidence of deeper learning, I had come to know many of the students, particularly the interview participants. These eight students were assigned pseudonyms for this report in order to protect their identities.

When describing student responses in the learning journals, another dilemma arose regarding identifying students. The majority of student responses that were of interest to this study came from the learning journals of the eight interview participants. However, occasionally to contrast or corroborate other accounts, I included data collected from the learning journals of students that were not selected for interviews. Because it seemed to complicate the presentation of the data to mention students by name only once in the study or when they did not exemplify the experiences in question, I made a decision to name only the interview participants. I believe that this decision makes the study more readable without distracting from or altering the data.

## My Connection to the Study

Part of doing qualitative research in educational settings is exploring one's own preconceived ideas and subjectivities (Peshkin, 1988) to expose any possible bias. One of my areas of subjectivity in this study is how close I am to the subject matter. I have been an adult language student in many classrooms and have been an instructor in college and community settings for almost as long. My enthusiasm for this subject matter runs deep.

I knew I wanted to be a language teacher from the first moment I began working as a teaching assistant (TA) in graduate school. My very first week on campus, I stepped into my own classroom, suddenly transformed from student to teacher. I remember feeling exhilarated while teaching. I also remember feeling exhausted and often baffled by my students' reactions to the material. My impetus to continue teaching was that I truly cared about studying languages and felt honored to have the chance to share that passion with my students.

A colleague of mine told me recently that she taught her first class as a TA before she attended her first class in her graduate program. I taught my first class the morning after attending my first graduate lecture. We were given a textbook, a syllabus template and told to speak entirely in the target language. Then we were sent on our way. We just figured things out as we went along. According to Wurdinger and Carlson (2010), most college faculty do not take any pedagogy courses while in their doctoral programs and then subsequently use an ineffective lecture format in their teaching. The pedagogy class I did eventually take as a TA was not necessarily geared toward adult learners, but took a blanket approach to methods, lumping all learners of all ages and all contexts into one category. I know my experience with methods was not unique. Clearly, graduate students who plan to teach language at the college level are in need of guidance in the teaching methods that are best suited to adult students.

Another colleague, after reading a portion of this study, told me that despite being a TA for several years and teaching as an assistant professor at a liberal arts college for two years, she had never read the standards for foreign language teaching. How many of us can say that we teach first and second year courses but have no knowledge of the standards, or of adult learning processes, or of current best practices in teaching languages?

Having taught language in community and corporate settings, at universities, a community college and a small liberal arts college in the US, I know the frustrations and challenges of the language classroom. In fact, it was my quest to understand my post-secondary students that led me, as a Master's-level instructor, to return to school and pursue a doctorate in Adult Education. I wanted to know not just how to promote proficiency in the language, but also how to promote personal growth and development through language study. I wanted to guide my own students through the same kind of life-changing language study that I had experienced.

I have written this book with a group of readers in mind: those who teach the early levels of languages other than English in a post-secondary setting. Regardless of the particular language you teach, your years of experience teaching or the kind of institution in which you teach, I hope you will see your own students' experiences reflected here and feel empowered to apply adult learning theory in your own teaching.

# 2 Adult Learning Theory

The study of adult learning and development is a field of study with a range of theories and approaches that seek to define it; there is no one prevailing or dominant theory in the field (Elias & Meriam, 2005). This broad range can be attributed to the breadth of the field, the richness of adult experience and the number of other fields of study upon which adult learning theory draws. This rich and varied tradition explores psychological, social and systemic factors in adult learning, applying knowledge gained through multiple other fields to the specific study of how adults are educated and how they learn and develop over their lifespan. Because of the overlap of content, the field is most often associated with education, human resources and other settings where adults work and learn. In this chapter, I will explore some of the foundations of adult learning theory and discuss how the concepts are relevant to the language classroom.

## The Need for Adult Learning Theory

Our work in the language department tends to be informed by the material we teach, rather than by the students we teach. In language departments where I have taught, for example, my colleagues have been specialists in regional literature, cultural and historical studies, and linguistics. While all of us had some exposure to teaching methods in graduate school, our teaching is generally informed by our respective fields. Those of us who teach the lower-level language classes tend to draw our ideas about how and what to teach from the second language acquisition stream of scholarship.

As valuable as the literature on second language acquisition has been to the practice of language teaching, its contribution has been to describe how the content (a second language) is acquired by learners. The role of the learner as an individual and a member of a social group is minimized, thus reducing them to a 'language learning machine' (Pennycook, 2001: 143). In contrast, the field of adult education describes the learners themselves and thus has the potential to enhance the teaching of languages to adults in any setting. I argue that it is essential for those of us who teach college students to become more familiar with adult education, learning and development. This familiarity will improve our practice as we balance a dual focus on teaching our content well while also giving our students the tools they need to develop personally.

In my own professional practice, I find myself often asking questions like, how do my adult students grow into global citizens through language study? How can I present the content in a way that is not only rigorous and effective, but also promotes lifelong learning and intercultural connection? How can I ensure that adults in my lower-level language classes get the maximum benefit from the study of languages even if they do not continue their study long enough to reach fluency? These are all questions that adult learning theory can help answer.

Recalling that (a) it takes around 600 hours of language study to reach conversational competence and (b) most adult learners do not go on to make that large investment of time and energy, adult learning theory provides us hope that students in our language classes will take away something vital to their personal development, even if they do not reach fluency. This chapter is an outline of some adult learning models and is intended as an introduction to some key people and concepts in order to inform subsequent discussions. Here I describe in more depth the major frameworks of adult learning including experiential learning, self-directed learning, transformative learning, critical pedagogy and the effects of adult learning on individuals.

## Experiential Learning

One of the main threads in adult learning theory is the idea that experience is the fundamental source of education. Beginning with John Dewey, progressive educators began to reexamine the traditional tenets of education and realize they were ineffective with adults (Elias & Merriam, 2005). In 1938, the year that Dewey published the book *Experience and Education*, it was understood that desks, chalkboards and memorization may have had a place in preparing young learners for their future roles, but adults operated under a completely different set of assumptions. To start, adults came into their education already possessing a wealth of related experiences. Whereas it was widely accepted that children, new to the world, required classroom exposure in order to prepare for future life experiences, adults in a classroom already had the experiences. Therefore, such adults are not preparing for the future, but rather making sense of the past and present.

This reconceptualization of the relationship between experience and education was revolutionary in the early parts of the twentieth century. Nearly a hundred years later, the prevailing wisdom of education for children and adults is that people of all ages learn best through experience. However, the seeds for experiential learning as a fundamental methodology were sown by adult educators.

In the context of a language classroom, this can be a radical concept as well. For adults, language learning is not just preparation for some future opportunity to speak or for a more advanced class. Adults have likely already traveled, met people from other cultures, experienced prejudice and built relationships. Not only have they had relevant experiences in the past, they are likely to have relevant experiences while enrolled in a language course. So, if we believe that experience is education, then what we do in our classrooms cannot just be preparation for some future intercultural experience, but must, in fact, engage the collective experiences of our adult students. Our language classes, even at the lower levels, are not only teaching adults to communicate and interact in the target language, but also to reexamine and make sense of their previous and current experiences. The wealth of experience that adults bring to the classroom is one of their greatest assets.

If we concede that experience is fundamental to adult education, then can we also say that any adult who has had a significant number of experiences with a particular concept would be considered an expert in that concept? Obviously, the answer is no. While learning is built on experience, all experience, in and of itself, does not lead to learning. As John Dewey says, 'The belief that all genuine education comes about through experience does not mean that all experiences are genuinely or equally educative' (1938/1998: 13). It is possible for students to have experiences that lead to no long-term learning of any kind. The experiential learning process involves reflecting and revisiting experiences in order to draw conclusions and make meaning.

The role of the adult educator, therefore, is to carefully construct course activities that not only draw on adult students' existing experiences, but also help to make those experiences educational (Moon, 2004). Kolb's (1984) experiential learning cycle is a useful guide for educators in curriculum development. This model overcomes what Kolb perceived to be notable deficiencies in prior conceptualizations of the learning process. First, Kolb noted that purely psychological descriptions of learning that emphasize the internal, psychological processes seemed to exclude the environment around the learner. Instead, learning became an inherently personal endeavor unrelated to experience. Second, in learning theories that accounted for the environmental input, such as in the behaviorism models, this input was reduced to a stimulus that produced a reaction in the learner. The interaction between learner and environment in previous learning models was one-way, while Kolb's model allowed the learner to experience the world, make sense of that experience, and then return to the world to put the learning into practice.

The learning cycle described in Kolb's theory has four parts. The first stage is Concrete Experience (CE), or actually participating and gaining an experience. Following Concrete Experience is the stage of Reflective Observation (RO), in which the learner reflects on the experience, asks questions and discusses issues related to the experience. Then, through the stage called Abstract Conceptualization (AC), the learner connects the experience to larger theories, ideas or other knowledge. Finally, in the stage called Active Experimentation (AE), the learner applies what they have learned in similar or new situations. This type of learning is cyclical, meaning that the Active Experimentation of one learning cycle could produce the Concrete Experience for the next learning cycle.

In a language classroom, there is no limit to the ways this cycle could be effectively used. As described in Figure 2.1, when teaching communicative skills, a CE classroom activity might be an interpretive task where learners listen to or read a text in the target language. Through guided activities designed to help students notice and reflect on specific language features, the class engages in RO individually or as a group, working through the text and asking key questions about the text. In the AC stage, the features brought to light in the previous stage might be compared to grammar rules or other texts with which the learners are familiar. Finally, in AE, the students construct their own oral or written language using the experiential knowledge they have gained.

Experiential learning could also be well-suited to culture teaching. Imagine asking adult language students to attend a community event or watch a film that takes place in the target culture. That experience could be simply an interesting experience with no further exploration. However, if the instructor frames that experience as one stage in the learning cycle and guides learners through the steps, that experience becomes an opportunity for personal growth.

If we define learning as Kolb did, as 'the process whereby knowledge is created through the transformation of experience' (1984: 41), then the role of the language educator is to provide adult students with as many opportunities as possible to experience and reflect on language and culture, and then to make abstract connections and actively experiment with that language and culture. This cycle will lead our students to be able to transform their experiences into knowledge – not just their experiences in our classroom, but also their experiences in the world as adults who will inevitably come into contact with other languages and cultures. Encouraging

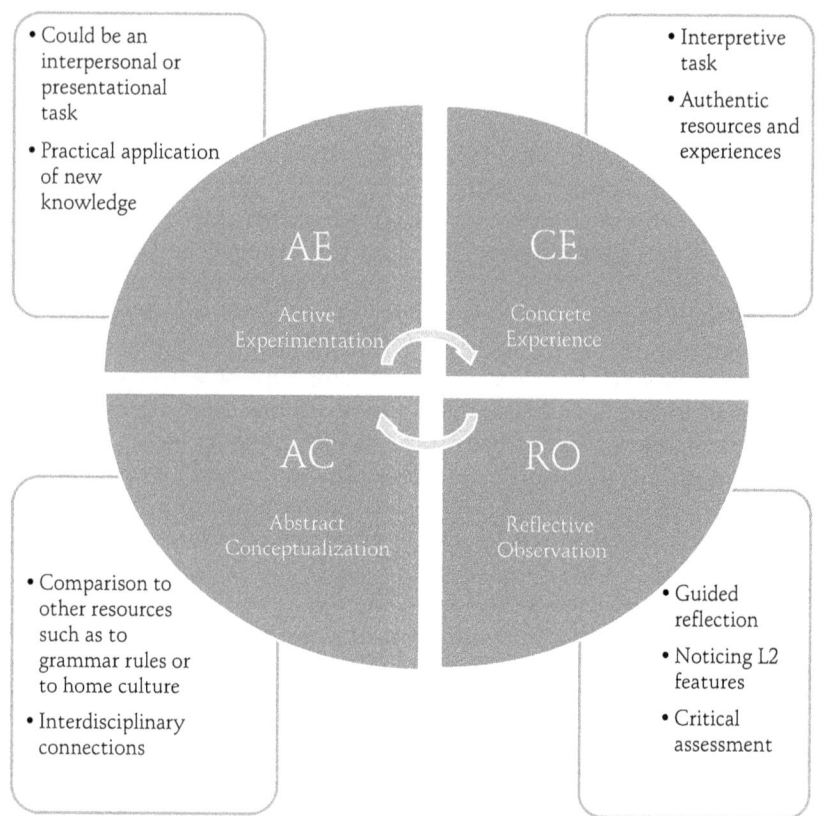

**Figure 2.1** The experiential learning cycle applied to language learning adapted from Kolb (1984).

adult language students to master this type of learning produces lifelong learners who can readily make sense of their life experiences long after they have left the classroom.

## Self-Directed Learning

The idea that adults have a strong concept of self and are motivated to learn entirely intrinsically is one of the more controversial claims of adult education scholarship. According to Knowles' theory of andragogy (Knowles *et al.*, 2005), adults are self-directed learners. This means that students choose to take language classes and are motivated to learn because they already believe that language study will be useful to them in real-world settings.

I believe that most students I have taught over the years would agree that knowing a second language would be quite useful. Yet, when these same students are confronted with the Herculean task of studying for years to achieve fluency in another language, their learning becomes much less motivated. I know that many adults do study languages voluntarily, but most of my students study Spanish as a required course in their college career. They must take my course in order to graduate. Clearly, college students taking a required course cannot be expected to engage in self-directed learning to communicate in a language they are not intrinsically motivated to learn.

So, while adults may be self-directed learners inherently, that quality does not apply equally to all subjects for all learners. Part of my job as a language teacher is to discover what my adult students are motivated to learn. Where does their inherent self-directed learning lead them? Perhaps I can harness my student-athlete's propensity for self-directed learning by asking her to do a target language project on a famous athlete in her sport. A music major becomes more self-directed in his learning when I use songs and lyrics to provide concrete examples of culture and grammatical constructions. Project-based learning (PBL) has in fact emerged as a classroom practice that engages adult students' natural disposition toward self-directed learning by allowing adults to choose topics for which they feel intrinsically motivated. PBL encourages students to become progressively more creative and autonomous in their learning (Stoller, 2006). Autonomy in language learning (Benson, 2013; Holec, 1979) is closely related to self-directed learning, implying less teacher intervention and more ability on the part of the student to monitor and assess his or her own work.

While self-directed learning is undeniably an important topic within adult learning, there are differences in how scholars and practitioners understand the term. On one hand, prominent voices in the field such as Eduard Lindeman and Malcolm Knowles describe adults as inherently self-directed. Adults simply *are* self-directed and adult educators should work with adult students to facilitate the students' own learning goals. On the other hand, scholars such as Kegan (1994) take this concept to task as being less a foundation of adult education and more a byproduct of the same. According to Kegan, the self-direction we seek from adult learners is actually an advanced level of intellectual maturity that we can promote in our classrooms, but not hope to achieve unless the learners find themselves at such a point in their overall development. In a critique of adults as self-directed learners, Kegan cuts to the heart of the issue:

After all, what *is* this demand for 'self-directed learning'? Does it consist in a set of trainable skills or does it, yet again, reflect something more like a qualitative order of mental complexity that would in turn permit such skills? The goal of 'self-directed learning' may represent a far greater convergence than that composed by several scholars in the single field of adult education. It may reflect a culturewide convergence, a culturewide curriculum calling across every frequented area of adult life... (1994: 274)

According to Kegan, instructors should be more concerned with adult students' overall personal growth and development so that, over time, they will reach a maturational stage of self-direction. With this in mind, this study examines adult development within the language classroom.

## Transformative Learning

Transformative learning theory describes the learning process that takes place when adults reevaluate previously held beliefs and attitudes and begin to interpret experiences in a new way. While not yet widely applied in language classrooms, there is a strong connection between transformative learning and deep language learning.

A dichotomy exists in the kinds of learning that adults experience. In the context of a foreign language classroom, students learn the content: discrete units of grammar, vocabulary and cultural information. They also learn the skills necessary to use the content in linguistic contexts such as conversations or written communications. Mezirow (1991) refers to this learning of content and skills as instrumental. Alternatively, students may experience another kind of learning in a foreign language class that Mezirow describes as transformative learning. Transformative learning is also referred to as transformational learning; for the purposes of this study, the two terms are synonymous. In transformative learning, the student is able to critically reflect on his or her own meaning perspectives, or assumptions about how the world works, and interpret experience from a new perspective.

### Meaning perspectives

It has been said that we do not see things as *they* are, rather we see them as *we* are. Viewing the world through the lens of one's beliefs, assumptions, experiences, and linguistic and cultural norms is referred to by Mezirow (1991) as a meaning perspective. The tendency to see the world from a fixed perspective, according to certain expectations, is how individuals make sense out of their experiences. Mezirow (1997) also uses the term habit of mind to refer to meaning perspectives. 'An example of a habit of mind is ethnocentrism, the predisposition to regard others outside one's own group as inferior' (p. 6). What better place to address ethnocentrism than in a language and culture classroom?

The information a student takes in through her senses is filtered through the lens of her meaning perspective. New knowledge that is consistent with her previous expectations is accepted and integrated. New knowledge that is not consistent with her meaning perspective will suffer one of several fates: (a) It may be discarded, dismissed as an aberration or impossibility and filtered out by the lens of her meaning perspective, (b) the new input may be modified to better fit into the preexisting worldview of the student, interpreted according to the existing meaning perspective or (c) it may cause a conflict between the previous frame of reference and the new information. If this conflict is explored, it can lead to a transformation of the student's perspective.

Several sociolinguistic elements contribute to the formation of one's meaning perspective including social norms and roles, cultural and language codes, common sense as a cultural system, and ethnocentrism (Mezirow, 1991). All of these elements allow people to live within their native language and the structures of their culture and readily discard any input that does not fit in their system. The common language of a group of people bonds them into a 'dialogic community' (56) that shares meaning through common symbols. Becoming socialized in the codes and assumptions of one's native language and culture is a normal part of childhood and serves to mold young people into productive members of their group. Sometimes referred to as the ideology of a social group, meaning is passed on to younger members of a group through this social indoctrination.

> Each of us 'breathes in' an ideology as we live and grow in our society. Each person takes on or takes in the prevailing set of assumptions about reality – the meaning perspective – of the particular social group that provides the immediate context for his or her socialization... Through the process of enculturation, a person develops a self-identity and a self-interest, both of which reproduce the reality framing and value assumptions of the social group and the larger society. (Kennedy, 1990: 99)

Because of the nature of first language and culture acquisition, the concept of meaning perspective is intertwined with early language acquisition. Some children grow up in environments where they are exposed to more than one linguistic and cultural perspective. Bi- and multilingual children, whose meaning perspective has integrated the values and assumptions of at least two frameworks, are better at some kinds of problem-solving than monolinguals and have greater metalinguistic awareness (Bialystok, 1988; Fromkin et al., 2003). Metalinguistic awareness is an individual's consciousness about language and how language works, about issues such as the arbitrary relationship between sound and meaning or the possibilities for language use. Metalinguistic awareness gained by children through second language learning results in higher proficiency with written language and improved ability to manipulate linguistic structures (Demont, 2001). A lack of metalinguistic awareness may cause an individual to believe that his own native language is the only one that is logical. However, bi- and multilingual people are more likely to recognize that all languages are based on arbitrary symbols and complex grammars.

For monolingual adults entering an elementary foreign language course, metalinguistic awareness may be difficult to develop. A native English speaker's common sense, which is a cultural construct embedded in his meaning perspective, tells him that shoe is the only possible word for what he wears on his feet; 'zapato' in Spanish and '鞋' in Chinese just do not feel right. Teaching an adult a new item of vocabulary is not simply memorizing the sound, spelling and arbitrary relationship to an idea. More challenging is the task of increasing that adult's metalinguistic awareness and broadening her worldview so that the possibility of a new, equally valid word can be integrated into his meaning perspective.

### Perspective transformation

According to Mezirow, perspective transformation is the hallmark of transformative learning:

> Perspective transformation is the process of becoming critically aware of how and why our assumptions have come to constrain the way we perceive, understand, and feel about our world; changing these structures of habitual expectation to make possible a more inclusive, discriminating, and integrating perspective; and, finally, making choices or otherwise acting upon these new understandings (1991: 167).

Transformative learning theory outlines a ten-step process through which individuals undergo perspective transformation. The steps Mezirow identifies are:

(1) A disorienting dilemma
(2) Self-examination with feelings of guilt or shame

(3) A critical assessment of epistemic, sociocultural, or psychic assumptions
(4) Recognition that one's discontent and the process of transformation are shared and that others have negotiated a similar change
(5) Exploration of options for new roles, relationships, and actions
(6) Planning a course of action
(7) Acquisition of knowledge and skills for implementing one's plans
(8) Provisional trying of new roles
(9) Building of competence and self-confidence in new roles and relationships; and
(10) A reintegration into one's life on the basis of conditions dictated by one's new perspective. (1991: 168-9)

Other researchers have conceptualized the process of perspective transformation in different ways. What all of the models have in common is a movement from the disorienting dilemma to critical reflection, then to conscious action, and finally to integration, resulting in a new, broader meaning perspective.

The initial stages of perspective transformation require an individual to recognize a conflict between an experience and her own meaning perspective, and then to reflect on and examine that conflict. These early stages are crucial to perspective transformation (Mezirow, 1991). The facilitator, whether a teacher or supervisor, can inhibit perspective transformation by stifling or ignoring critical reflection, or can promote the transformation by creating an environment where critical reflection is encouraged and valued. In a classroom setting, a student, recognizing a conflict, may begin to ask questions during class discussion or exhibit other indicators. Mezirow lists some signs or indicators that perspective transformation is, in fact, taking place in an individual. These indicators include:

> Seeking assistance from a wider variety of sources of knowledge; taking a more critical stance; looking at helpers as resources for finding one's own answers rather than as authorities who will provide the answers; testing boundaries and assumptions; actively looking for patterns of behavior and avoidance in oneself; greater awareness of emotions, physical states, intuition, and dream symbolism; and searching for forms of assistance compatible with one's learning style. (193-4)

By looking for these and other indicators, an instructor who is familiar with the process of perspective transformation can create an environment where the early stages of the process, namely the disorienting dilemma and critical reflection, are supported, validated and encouraged.

Many fields of study include the concept of meaning perspectives, the underlying determiner of how individuals interpret experience, although this idea is often referred to in other ways. Whorf (1956) explores the concept of language structures and the effect these structures have on constraining people's interpretations of reality. Kuhn (1962) refers to paradigms and Foucault (1972) used the term episteme. Mezirow (1991) includes the term schemata in his discussion of meaning perspectives. In language assessment, it is considered valuable to activate a student's general schemata (O'Malley & Valdez Pierce, 1996), or framework of background knowledge and expectations that can help him interpret a text. However, a student's schemata are culture-specific and, for second language learners, new knowledge may clash with the existing schemata causing conflict between the student's meaning perspective and the set of assumptions inherent in the text. This conflict can be the basis of the experience that transformative learning theory terms the disorienting dilemma.

## Disorienting dilemma

The disorienting dilemma is the event that precipitates perspective transformation. When a student is confronted with evidence that conflicts with his or her existing meaning perspective, a sense of imbalance may challenge the student's sense of order and meaning. This event may lead to a process of self-examination and critical reflection often experienced as intense and emotional. 'A disorienting dilemma that begins the process of transformation also can result from an eye-opening discussion, book, poem, or painting or from efforts to understand a different culture with customs that contradict our own previously accepted presuppositions' (Mezirow, 1991: 168).

In an adult foreign language classroom, the conflict caused when students encounter a language and culture different from their own may cause a disorienting dilemma. Students with little previous contact with other groups may especially struggle to make sense of the clash of symbols, values and assumptions as they learn to speak and act in a new way.

A disorienting dilemma may come from other sources beside the classroom environment. Students' experiences in life can have a deep impact on their learning (King, 2000; Mezirow, 1991). Three categories of dilemmas are identified (Mezirow, 1991): self-induced, induced by life circumstances and induced by other people like a teacher or friend. How the process begins is not as important as how it is continued and promoted through subsequent experiences. In reality, it is likely a mix of experiences both within and outside of the classroom that help to bring a student to the disorienting dilemma wherein she questions her assumptions about reality. In the context of adult language education, King (2000) found that classroom activities have a more prominent role than life experiences in promoting transformative learning.

We as language instructors are not the sole source of perspective transformation, but the choices we make in our classrooms do have a significant impact on our students' learning outcomes. Therefore, understanding the sorts of practices that promote perspective transformation is essential.

## Critical reflection

Critical reflection has been established as a crucial element in certain kinds of learning, especially for adult learners (Mezirow, 1991; Kitchener & King, 1990). Scholars have categorized the kinds of learning dependent on critical reflection in a number of ways. When Säljö (1979) asked adults what they understood by learning, their answers fell into two general categories. First, they responded that learning is the simple acquisition of information or behavior. In a foreign language class, that would be the equivalent of learning the content and skills. The second category of learning that adults described in Säljö's study was more complex. This learning, which Säljö refers to as real learning or understanding, requires adults to make sense of information in relation to the real world and to themselves. It is a process by which adults acquire a new point of view, reorganize beliefs and ideas or reevaluate assumptions. This reorganization and reevaluation requires adult learners to critically examine their own beliefs, values and behaviors in the light of new information. The difference between the two categories of learning is the presence of critical reflection.

Foreign language education researchers have also discussed critical reflection. Knutson (2006) describes a process of developing cross-cultural awareness based on students' critical reflection on differences and similarities between the home and target cultures. Brady (2006) expounds a concept which he called dialogically engaged language communal communication in which critical awareness is crucial to deep learning.

Researchers have found that certain kinds of activities foster critical reflection and perspective transformation in an adult classroom. According to Cranton (2006), these include consciousness-raising activities where students become critically aware of their own and others' beliefs and begin to question familiar roles; activities that involve experiential learning where the student ventures into the real world to explore the subject matter; and journaling and arts-based activities. Group work, also called collaborative learning, may foster transformative learning by giving students a space where they can share feelings and reactions and reflect on new experiences (Pilling-Cormick, 1997). Brookfield (1990), Tisdell and Thompson (2007) and Guy (2007) recommend using pop culture media, and Freire (1970/2000) emphasized the importance of dialogue. Sharing personal struggles and experience was fundamental to the experience of perspective transformation in consciousness-raising groups during the women's movement (Hart, 1990). Nevertheless, student reactions to collaborative learning may initially be unfavorable (Hughes Wilhelm, 1997).

The body of literature dealing specifically with perspective transformation in foreign language education is small, and much of this literature is theoretical in nature (see Foster, 1997; Goulah, 2006). However, the empirical research conducted on the topic of transformation in language education indicates that perspective transformation is prevalent in adult language classrooms (see Buttaro & King, 2001; Johnson & Mullins Nelson, 2010; King, 2000).

## Classroom connections

Describing students' attitudes and motivations in language study can be a valuable predictor of success in the language classroom. Clearly, social and psychological factors are dynamic and can be influenced (Gardner, 2001). Can teachers improve students' potential for success by helping to shape their attitudes about language study or about the target culture? If transformative learning has the potential to alter students' perceptions of reality, their patterns of thinking and the way they interpret experience and interact with the world, then it is reasonable to conclude that social and psychological factors can change as students' perspectives are transformed. Since these factors are important to student success in language study, then it is also possible to conclude, as Pennycook (2001) did, that transformative learning can affect students' linguistic proficiency by altering social and psychological factors like acculturation and motivation. Such a conclusion gives transformative learning a place of high importance in the communicative foreign language classroom. In fact, Citron (2001) who drew on these and other aspects of second language research, proposes that 'having a mind that is open to other ways of looking at the world might help one to learn a new language' (105).

Transformative learning theory proposes that certain kinds of learning can open students' minds to new ways of viewing and interacting with the world. Citron argues that 'having a perspective that is not limited by one's own cultural and linguistic experiences, but rather is open to the contrasting cultural and linguistic patterns of other peoples can aid one in acquiring a second language' (2001: 111). Therefore, promoting transformative learning in foreign language classrooms is an important step in promoting linguistic and communicative competence. Whether or not communicative competence is an intended outcome of instruction, clearly students achieve greater success in foreign language learning when they also possess higher levels of ethno-relativity (Citron, 2001), increased integrative motivation and more positive attitudes toward the target language group.

## The Effects of Adult Learning

John Dewey (1938/1998) writes that adult education should have a developmental and moral effect on its participants. Dewey's contemporary, Eduard Lindeman exclaims that 'education is life – not a mere preparation for an unknown kind of future living' (1961: 4). In our language classrooms, according to these fathers of adult education, adult students should leave not only more conversant in a language other than English, but also more morally developed and aware of the opportunities life presents for learning about language and culture. Why do I plan my language classes with adult development in mind? Because I want my students to know much more than how to read, write, speak and listen to the language. I want my students to become ambassadors between cultures, to engage the world in which they live.

In fact, as an adult in my classroom, the activities of the classroom impact me, and I am also a beneficiary of adult development. Teachers are the facilitators and guides through the learning process because they have experienced and continue to pursue the same learning processes. Like many language teachers, I became an instructor because I loved learning about language and culture. As a teacher, I continue to learn and grow alongside my students.

Indeed, according to Kegan (1994), the intellectual development of adults is not just a desirable byproduct of education or the happy fulfillment of teachers' own hopes for their students or for themselves. Rather, adult students' learning is essential for them to function at high levels in a complex and ever-changing world.

As adult language students develop, they become increasingly more aware of and open to differences between and within cultures (Johnson & Mullins Nelson, 2010). Supporting cultural awareness and the ability to critically reflect on difference, Chávez et al. (2003) present a model of individual diversity development that emphasizes critical reflection in order to progress from one level to the next. In this model, shown in Figure 2.2, a student begins by being unaware of foreign perspectives, knowing only his own. As he progresses, he passes through a dualistic phase, which is inherently ethnocentric. In this phase, the student perceives his own and the foreign perspective to be at odds, and feels the need to choose sides. The student

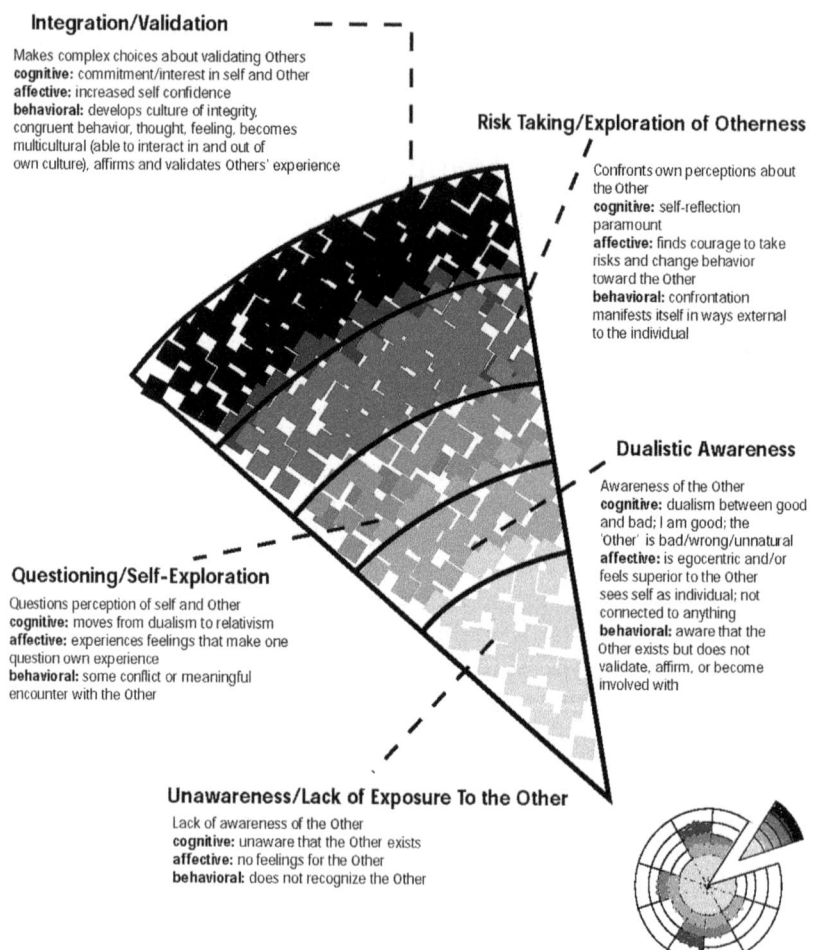

**Figure 2.2** Learning to Value the 'Other': A Framework of Individual Diversity Development. Source: Chavez, A.F. et al. (2003) Learning to value the 'Other': A framework of individual diversity development. *Journal of College Student Development* 44 (4), 459, figure 1. © 2003 by the American College Personnel Association. Reprinted with permission of John Hopkins University Press.

takes a cognitive stance in favor of their own perspective, categorizing the Other as wrong or unnatural. As they increase their understanding of the relative nature of difference, students begin to question their previous assumptions and explore their own experiences. This phase is generally marked by a meaningful encounter with the Other. Moving into a phase of exploration, change begins to be externally visible as the student begins to take risks and change his behavior. Critical reflection is especially vital in this phase in order to make sense of the internal changes and manifest them externally. Students in the final phase of this model are able to critically evaluate aspects of both their own and foreign perspectives, making choices about what works best for them.

While a diversity development model may be too prescriptive to meet with the approval of scholars such as Kegan (1994), who emphasize the mental complexities inherent in genuine intellectual development, it provides a useful framework for educators who want to assess student development as a result of learning a new language. As language instructors well know, opportunities to explore diversity are abundant in a language classroom.

## Conclusion

Adult learning theory provides a basis for understanding how students grow and develop in the language classroom. Learning models such as the experiential learning cycle, self-directed learning and transformative learning explain learning processes that are linked to language learning. As a result of adult learning in the language classroom, students develop intellectually and in their awareness and appreciation of diversity.

# 3 Adult Language Education

In Chapter 2, I examined adult learning and development through the lens of language education. In this chapter, I will switch sides, examining in more detail the teacher's role in the classroom rather than the learners' experiences. I will discuss some of the foundations of language teaching and draw clear connections to adult education. While the terminology is quite different, the two fields deal with many of the same issues about how to organize and teach content, and assess student outcomes.

## Foreign Language Teaching Standards

In the Standards for Foreign Language Learning (ACTFL, n.d.), five concepts are emphasized as the core principles of language instruction: communication, cultures, connections, comparisons and communities.

> **Communication** is at the heart of second language study, whether the communication takes place face-to-face, in writing, or across centuries through the reading of literature. Through the study of other languages, students gain a knowledge and understanding of the **cultures** that use that language and, in fact, cannot truly master the language until they have also mastered the cultural contexts in which the language occurs. Learning languages provides **connections** to additional bodies of knowledge that may be unavailable to the monolingual English speaker. Through **comparisons** and contrasts with the language being studied, students develop insight into the nature of language and the concept of culture and realize that there are multiple ways of viewing the world. Together, these elements enable the student of languages to participate in multilingual **communities** at home and around the world in a variety of contexts and in culturally appropriate ways. (3)

These standards frame foreign language education as the process of exposing students not only to a new way of speaking, but also to a new way of thinking, acting and of viewing the world. With an emphasis on social roles and multiple cultural perspectives, the five principles established by the standards seem to encourage adult development through language study.

It is interesting to note that these standards do not specifically detail particular technical aspects of language (such as tense, mood or declension) that students should learn. In fact, the Council of Europe's (2014) Common Reference Levels (a set of documents comparable to ACTFL (2012) proficiency guidelines that distinguish different levels of language learners' communicative ability) do not reference specific lexical or grammatical components of language, but rather focus on the larger issues of what learners can do in the target language, how they can meet their own needs and engage in interaction using the language.

In particular, this approach contrasts with much of what is produced in applied linguistics and second language acquisition (SLA) research. While the exact way specific lexical items or grammatical concepts are acquired by learners in ideal settings is an important focus for SLA research, the standards for language teaching and language proficiency ignore those details altogether, looking instead at the larger issues of whole language use.

As I mentioned in the previous chapter, most language teachers would draw on linguistics and second language acquisition (SLA) research in framing their teaching practice. After all, these are the fields that use scientific inquiry to investigate and describe language and how languages are learned. And yet, based on the frequent attention given to the gap between SLA and language teaching (Lantolf & Pohner, 2014), it seems that language teachers are often unable to apply the knowledge gleaned through SLA research. According to Block (2000), 'much of what is done under the rubric of SLA is not particularly relevant to language teachers and is not really applicable to the day-to-day language teaching and learning which goes on in classrooms' (130).

So, if SLA research is not readily applicable to postsecondary teachers' actual classrooms, what other fields of study inform our work? Scholarly literature on language teaching and learning has also enjoyed close ties to the fields of education and psychology (Borg, 2003; Richards & Rogers, 2001). Any research that describes learning, language, culture or human interaction could reasonably be applied to language teaching. Although there is a growing body of classroom-oriented research on language teaching and learning, the gap between research and practice persists.

For the foreseeable future, it is the standards and not the research that will play the largest role in shaping curriculum and classroom practice.

## Teaching Methods

A substantial body of literature exists on specific foreign language techniques and methods that are most effective for specific learning outcomes. Students and teachers often have conflicting ideas about which methods are most effective (Brown, 2009), but there is no shortage of evidence of well-established best practices, such as exposing students to the most authentic language and culture possible (Abrams *et al.*, 2006; Di Carlo, 1994) and including the use of authentic media texts such as film and television and contact with native speakers and communities (Byram & Kramsch, 2008; Kramsch, 1993). Many of these same activities also promote critical reflection and can be catalysts for transformative learning in addition to learning content (Guy, 2007; Tisdell & Thompson, 2007).

Over the last century, new foreign language teaching approaches, methods and techniques have found their way into college classrooms. *Approach, method, technique* and a plethora of other terms which are often used interchangeably to refer to how teachers present content and guide students (Kumaravadivelu, 2006) have different implications. Brown (2002) defined *approach* as a large over-arching set of principles that teachers use to guide decisions about how class will be conducted; 'a set of assumptions dealing with the nature of language, learning, and teaching' (9). A *method* is a set of prescriptive rules for instruction based on the principles of the approach, and *technique* refers to the specific activities or functions that are generated as the method and approach are applied in the classroom. In addition to *technique*, I also use the terms *classroom practice* and *classroom activity* to describe the specific tasks, routines, assignments and other instructional techniques used in the classroom. Whether discussing methods, techniques or activities, all of these are rooted in a specific approach, or way of thinking about language instruction that guides the classroom.

In order to understand the techniques, practices and activities in a foreign language classroom, it is useful to examine the philosophical orientations that inform practice. Several recognized trends have historically dominated college classrooms. I will restrict my discussion, however, to two of particular relevance to both adult education and contemporary language teachers.

The first, the traditional approach, maintains a focus on language as content to be memorized and rigidly applied, instead of as a fluid skill or a perspective. The term 'traditional approach' is often used as a direct synonym for the grammar-translation method. However, for the purposes of this study, I also include another method that prioritizes language learning as the memorization and production of specific content, specifically, the audiolingual method. The traditional approach to language teaching is one that students throughout history, and in today's classrooms, will recognize from their personal experiences as language learners; workbooks, drills, repetition and memorization are its hallmarks.

The traditional approach to language teaching breaks language into discrete units of memorized information which are then presented to students, generally in their own native language, also called the home language or L1. Instruction takes place in the L1 focusing on the language skills of reading and writing. The foreign language, normally referred to as the target language or the L2, is not used for self-expression or communication, but rather to translate L2 texts into the L1.

The second approach is communicative language teaching, the paradigm that has dominated the last 30 years of research and is currently the standard in most classrooms. While the communicative approach is often used in a narrow way to describe just one of many related approaches that encourage communicative competence, I use the term to describe the multitude of interaction-based approaches that require students to understand and produce spontaneous language.

In contrast to the traditional approach, the communicative approach to language instruction teaches language for communication and exchange. This approach first came into view in the 1970s (Mitchell & Vidal, 2001) and has steadily gained prominence. Brown describes its distinguishing qualities as:

(1) Classroom goals are focused on all the components of CC [communicative competence] and not restricted to grammatical or linguistic competence.
(2) Language techniques are designed to engage learners in the pragmatic, authentic, functional use of language for meaningful purpose. Organizational language forms are not the central focus but rather aspects of language that enable the learner to accomplish those purposes.
(3) Fluency and accuracy are seen as complementary principles underlying communicative techniques. At times fluency may have to take on more importance than accuracy in order to keep learners meaningfully engaged in language use.
(4) In the communicative classroom, students ultimately have to use the language, productively and receptively, in unrehearsed contexts. (2007: 241)

Although the communicative approach is widely considered to be the current paradigm in language education theory and research, it is not employed universally in practice. Many classroom instructors still employ more traditional methods.

In Kumaravadivelu's (2006) categorization of method, he refers to traditional approaches to teaching as *language-centered*, communicative teaching as *learner-centered*, and methods such as the Natural Approach, that reject prescriptive functional and notional learning, as *learning-centered*, whereby learners acquire whatever language may be necessary to complete tasks and solve problems. In an important caveat, Kumaravadivelu points out that these categorical distinctions represent ideals, and not the realities of how real teachers in real classrooms employ the methods.

In this discussion, in a book based on classroom research, I prefer to focus on the realities of the classroom rather than the ideals of theory whenever possible. My use of two general categories, instead of three like Kumaravadivelu (2006) or many like Mitchell and Vidal (2001), reflects my analysis of the needs of real teaching situations. The most significant debate about how to teach language seems to revolve around whether we focus on form (grammar and accuracy) or function (communication and fluency) (Gallup Rodríguez, 2009). In practice, language teachers have tended to align themselves with one of these two sides while liberally borrowing from both. I believe that debate is accurately reflected in the categories of traditional and communicative language teaching.

## Adult education philosophies informing approach

The traditional, grammar-translation approach used in the Western world is an outgrowth of the liberal arts philosophy of education, which has its roots in ancient Greece and Rome, and where the goal is for the student to develop intellectually. Latin and ancient Greek were the languages thought most important for promoting intellectual development and increasing the learner's understanding of the classics in literature, philosophy and science (Brown, 2007). These languages are useful for reading and translating, but with no possibility to be used in a real-world context. For that reason, in the traditional liberal arts foreign language classroom, activities emphasize the skills of translation and reading and largely ignore the spoken language.

Historically, the goal of a liberal arts education was to educate the elite in order to produce a wiser class of rulers (Elias & Merriam, 2005). The focus was not on the practical application of knowledge (these future rulers would never need vocational training, after all), but rather on knowledge that contributed to the mental and moral capacity of the student. A modern liberal arts education for adults aims to produce an individual who is literate 'intellectually, morally, spiritually, and aesthetically' (33). The traditional method of teaching foreign languages would support this liberal arts program goal in two ways. First, adult students would learn the mechanical processes associated with language, such as conjugation and declension, and be familiar with language structures in general terms, thus increasing their understanding and appreciation of language and their metalinguistic awareness. Second, by acquiring the skills necessary to read texts from other languages, ancient or modern, and translate those texts into the L1, adult students can increase the pool of knowledge from which they draw. An adult student who finds herself in a program emphasizing the liberal arts philosophy will likely find that foreign language instruction is geared at improving her appreciation of foreign languages and of texts written in those languages, with little emphasis placed on the ability to use the foreign language to communicate in practical settings.

However, many adult students' motivations for taking foreign language classes do not match the assumptions of the liberal arts philosophy. For adult students, returning to school is often the solution to a problem, not the pursuit of knowledge for knowledge's sake. According to Knowles' model of andragogy (Knowles *et al.*, 2005), adults have a life-centered orientation to learning, meaning that in their lives, adult students discovered a need and have turned to education to fill that need. A life-centered orientation to learning is consistent with what researchers know about adult student motivations for going to college (Kasworm, 2003). In order to obtain a career or advance in a career, adults may choose college. Which foreign language they choose to study is also related to their career motivations (Uber Grosse *et al.*, 1998).

These student motivations are more closely related to the communicative approach that emphasizes authentic speech and real-world contexts. In a communicative classroom, the student learns language in order to use it in practical contexts, such as work or social settings. The progressive philosophy of adult education promotes learning for solving real-world problems. Elias and Merriam cite several principles of progressive adult education. First, progressive adult education broadens the view of the purpose of education, permitting and even 'advocating the introduction of the practical, pragmatic, and utilitarian into the curriculum' (2005: 62). This clearly resonates with the description of the communicative approach in terms of the 'pragmatic, authentic, functional use of language for meaningful purposes' (Brown, 2007: 241). Adult foreign language learning no longer needs to be purely for intellectual stimulation, but can exist as a practical pursuit with application in students' homes, workplaces and social settings.

A second principle of progressive adult education (Elias & Merriam, 2005) is to break away from previous teacher-centered educational philosophies and provide a new focus for education: the student. In order to create an atmosphere where students are actively participating and using the target language, it is essential for communicative language teachers to foster a student-centered environment where students' learning styles, preferences, experiences, and competencies are valued and acknowledged. In the communicative approach, lesson plans and course objectives are flexible enough to adjust in order to 'keep learners meaningfully engaged', as Brown (2007: 241) points out.

Another principle is the use of innovative methodologies that break from the liberal arts tradition. The use of innovative methodologies suggests a pragmatic application of techniques (meaning, do whatever works). Also important in progressive educational philosophy is the redefinition of the teacher-learner relationship. In the progressive classroom, the teacher becomes a facilitator instead of a gatekeeper. Both of the aforementioned principles of the progressive philosophy of adult education also describe the communicative approach to foreign language teaching.

Research on student motivations for pursuing higher education indicates that the liberal arts model with its traditional foreign language teaching methods may not be the most relevant approach for adults. Knowles et al. (2005), for instance, support a progressive philosophy of education when they describe adult students as interested in the practical application of knowledge. This falls in line with the communicative approach to language teaching.

Although the progressive philosophy in many ways informs the current paradigm of adult foreign language education, some institutions and faculty are reluctant to abandon the liberal arts philosophy, expressing dismay at the trend toward making foreign language education more focused on career or life application (see Corral & Patai, 2008).

## Organization of course content

All of the decisions that the instructor makes in order to organize the content into manageable units, along with decisions about how and when to teach what to whom, are of vital importance in creating an atmosphere where adult language learning is fostered. Of interest in this study are two related but distinct models for presenting content: the synthetic syllabus and the analytic syllabus (Beglar & Hunt, 2002).

When developing a synthetic syllabus, the instructor generally divides language into discrete units, verbs, nouns, tenses, etc. Then, certain units are grouped together to form lessons on grammar, vocabulary, culture or to teach about other categories of words. The words may be organized around a theme or grouped in some other way. The key to a synthetic syllabus is that the instructor knows in advance exactly what content will be taught and what students should learn. A synthetic syllabus is product-oriented. The content is driven by the instructor (or perhaps by the textbook author), not by the students or by the situation. The traditional approach to language teaching uses a synthetic syllabus.

In contrast, one of the innovations of the communicative approach to foreign language teaching is the analytic syllabus. This type of syllabus is a model for planning classroom activities centered on thematic units and real-world problem-solving, requiring students to use appropriate language for a situation, instead of teaching specific chunks of language with the hope that students will be able to apply it in a variety of situations. In a classroom using an analytic syllabus, the instructor will design a set of tasks or activities that require students to use the L2 and students will be responsible for discovering and acquiring the language they need to complete the tasks. An analytic syllabus requires students to make key decisions about what they need to learn in order to complete tasks.

While this model is closely linked with a classroom method known as task-based learning or a task-based instruction, there is some disagreement among scholars (Kumaravadivelu, 2006; Sheen, 2008) about whether the task-based approach falls under the umbrella of the communicative approach. For the purpose of this study, task-based instruction is considered a sub-category of communicative method due to its emphasis on intelligibility over accuracy in communication.

The distinction between synthetic and analytic syllabi is also discussed in Knowles' description (Knowles *et al.*, 2005) of the difference between the *content* and *process* models of adult program planning.

> The difference is this: in traditional education the teacher (or trainer or curriculum committee or somebody) decides in advance what knowledge or skill needs to be transmitted... This is a *content* model (or design)....The difference is not that one deals with content and the other does not; the difference is that the content model is concerned with transmitting information and skills, whereas the process model is concerned with providing procedures and resources for helping learners acquire information and skills. (2005: 115)

Clearly, the analytic syllabus is closely aligned with the process model. Both the analytic and process concepts focus less on *what* students learn and more on *how* they learn it by providing students with a framework that guides their learning while, ultimately, giving them autonomy over their learning experience. The analytic syllabus and the process model stand in contrast to the synthetic syllabus and the content model which both decide beforehand what specific discrete information students will learn, focusing more on the product rather than on the act of student learning.

## Student and teacher roles

The traditional approach to foreign language teaching employs a rigid classroom hierarchy where the teacher makes the key decisions about what to learn and when to learn it, and then the student learns what he is told. Freire (1970/2000) used the term *banking education* to refer to this process where the teacher attempts to transmit knowledge to the student. The student is simply a receptacle of the teacher's knowledge.

In a communicative classroom, the teacher's role is that of a facilitator and the student has a great deal of autonomy over what specific grammatical and lexical units to learn and how to interpret these units in context. The primary role of the instructor in a communicative classroom is to engage students in the processes of learning by guiding them and giving them feedback, allowing learners' wants and needs to guide instruction (Finney, 2002).

An adult student who desires autonomy over his or her own learning is referred to as a self-directed learner (Knowles *et al.*, 2005) even though, as discussed in Chapter 2, many researchers contest this characteristic of adult learners because not all exhibit this characteristic in the same way or to the same degree (Ross-Gordon, 2003). One interpretation of this term is that learners should be given control over course objectives and content, as would occur in a class using a purely analytic syllabus. Rachal (2002) points out, however, that this is often an impractical goal and rarely achieved.

In reality, a student who desires to be self-directed is one who will thrive in a learner-centered classroom where his or her ideas, experiences, learning styles and personal learning objectives are valued and included. In fact, Ross-Gordon's (2003) research indicates that adult students feel most comfortable in a classroom when their instructor is prepared, professional and clearly knowledgeable on the subject matter, as well as when he creates a classroom environment that is respectful of diverse backgrounds and abilities. Adult students want an instructor who is clearly capable of leading a class, not one who will defer to students on all decisions. This desire for a capable, professional classroom leader does not conflict with the idea of the learner-centered classroom. The learner-centered classroom is one of the defining characteristics of the communicative approach, representing a dramatic departure from the teacher-centered classroom associated with the traditional approach.

## Sources of knowledge about language

Another innovation of the communicative approach is the number of sources from which students draw their knowledge about a language. As mentioned previously, in the traditional approach, one of the focal points is on the translation of texts, especially of the classics. Students' only exposure to authentic language is likely to be classic literary texts written by noted authors. Aside from these texts, the instructor and authoritative grammar reference books are the student's primary sources of knowledge about the language. From an adult learning perspective, this represents a serious deficiency in the approach.

As discussed previously, Dewey (1938/1997) describes teaching and learning as the reconstruction of experience. From Dewey's perspective, a teacher's job is to provide adequate and engaging experiences from which students can learn. Knowles' (Knowles et al., 2005) theory of andragogy explains that experience is the richest source for adult learning. Lindeman (1961) explains that adult experience is the element separating the education of children from that of adults. Because of the ability of adult students to learn from experience, classroom practices that encourage experiential learning are most useful.

Recall that Kolb (1984) conceptualizes experiential learning as a process that involves four distinct phases: concrete experience, personal reflection, abstract conceptualization and active experimentation. This model is consistent with a technique for grammar instruction called inductive grammar that is associated with the communicative approach. The traditional method uses deductive reasoning to teach grammar, meaning that first students learn the rules and then apply those rules to a variety of sentences in different contexts. With inductive grammar techniques, students see or hear authentic examples of grammatical structures first, a phase Kolb describes as concrete experience. Then, the students work, through a variety of reflective and collaborative techniques, to explain the patterns in the examples they have seen. This is what Kolb calls personal reflection. The third step in inductive grammar begins with the teacher and student creating a rule, or generalizable category, that accurately describes the examples, and then students may apply their understanding of the grammatical concept in new contexts. In Kolb's experiential learning cycle, these are called abstract conception and active experimentation, respectively. Clearly, the communicative, inductive technique of grammar instruction allows adult students to harness their propensity to learn from experience, while the traditional, deductive technique does not.

In addition to Kolb's model, experiential learning has also come to mean any learning that occurs as a result of actually doing an activity in a real-world setting, such as a practicum, apprenticeship, field trip, service learning or job-shadowing (Cranton, 2006). Adults in particular are used to this type of learning from their real-world experiences as employees, family members and community members. Sometimes referred to as informal and incidental learning (Marsick & Watkins, 2001), adults pick up the skills and knowledge they need to succeed in life. How do our adult students learn what they need to be functional in life? They may have opportunities to learn in a classroom or training session, they may read books, and they may even have mentors. However, for the large majority of adults, they learn by doing, picking up skills as they go. This is a valuable skill in the classroom, harnessed through classroom practices that promote language learning in real-world settings, such as service learning and the use of authentic texts.

These two activities in particular, service learning and the use of authentic texts, are important innovations associated with the communicative approach. Since the communicative approach requires students to 'use the language, productively and receptively, in unrehearsed contexts' (Brown, 2007: 241), a variety of texts must be available to the student for practice, both written and aural, and representing different real-world contexts. The term *authentic texts* refers to texts in the L2 created for purposes other than classroom instruction, such as television commercials and informational brochures for products and services. Authentic texts are highly encouraged in the communicative approach and allow adults to use experience as a source of knowledge.

Service learning, embraced by communicative language teachers and supported by communicative principles, draws on two of the pillars of andragogy: (1) that adults learn best from experience and (2) that adult learning should be oriented to solving real-world problems. The communicative approach attempts to be more context-based by giving students opportunities to interact, discuss, observe and try new things in real-world or simulated real-world contexts.

## Moving Toward a New Approach

While the two approaches in the previous discussion represent the prevailing practice in adult language education, new ideas are emerging as to how and why we teach language. According to Brown (2002), the current trend in language education is toward a 'post-methods' or pragmatic approaches to instruction that select activities best aligned with specific learning objectives. Kumaravadivelu (2006) describes a post-methods language teaching reality that takes global and local factors into consideration, resulting in each classroom being shaped by the specific context and participants. Others (Beacco, 2011; Byram, 2008, 2010; Liddicoat & Scarino, 2013) would say we are moving toward a focus of global citizenship or intercultural competence as the main goal of language education. Zuengler and Miller (2006) describe the parallel research taking place on cognitive and, more recently, on sociocultural approaches.

In addition to studying language as the product of learning and as a tool for learning, much research exists on the social and psychological aspects of language learning. These external and internal processes related to language learning appear to have significant effects on language acquisition. Language acquisition does not occur in a vacuum, but rather is inextricably intertwined with who we are, how we perceive ourselves, and how we perceive others. I believe we are facing a new turn in how we, as a collective of researchers, teachers and learners, approach the teaching of languages at the postsecondary level. The following concepts are all contributing to the shaping of this new approach: sociocultural contexts, critical pedagogy, identity, motivation/investment and, perhaps most importantly, intercultural competence.

### Sociocultural contexts

The study of the sociocultural contexts of language learning is a relatively new field (Cross, 2010). Theorists may prescribe methodologies that 'conceive of teaching as little more than the sum of its parts – collections and patterns of behaviors and techniques' (434), but language instructors negotiate the sociocultural contexts of their own teaching, of their students' learning and of the classroom as an ecosystem. It has become clear that no one prescription for teaching and learning could possibly encompass all variables and all contexts.

The study of teachers and students as individuals, influenced and, in fact, defined by psychological and social factors, is broad and expanding

(Cross, 2010). Researchers and educators are becoming more aware of the fact that 'social activities and the language used to regulate them are structured and gain meaning in historically and culturally situated ways' (Johnson, 2006: 238). The language we teach is inextricable from the sociocultural contexts in which it is used. In addition, the teachers and students of a language are also rooted in specific yet evolving contexts with their own culturally situated identities (Knutson, 2006).

Any study of the sociocultural contexts of second language acquisition requires a rethinking of some key SLA assumptions about the role of language and culture in the classroom. Zuengler and Miller describe research on the sociocultural contexts of language learning in the following terms: 'These researchers focus not on language as input but as a resource for participation in the kinds of activities our everyday lives comprise. Participation in these activities is both the product and process of learning' (2006: 37–38).

## Critical pedagogy

Critical pedagogy is an approach to teaching that draws students' attention to the inequality present in existing structures and empowers them to act. Paolo Freire developed his theory of adult learning while teaching basic literacy to adults living in the slums of Brazil. He found that his adult students wanted to learn to read but also needed to see their own oppression from a critical perspective. Freire (1970/2000) terms this process of teaching basic literacy for transformation *conscientization*. He makes a distinction between conscientization and what he terms banking education, whereby the instructor uncritically transfers chunks of knowledge rather than making them the focus of critical reflection and awareness-raising.

Both transformative learning and critical pedagogy emphasize the importance of adult learners' engaging in critical reflection as part of the learning process. Given that close connection, many scholars in the field discuss aspects of both theoretical perspectives seemingly interchangeably. Brookfield, for example, writes about promoting the kind of critical thinking necessary for transformative learning (1987) as well as on the role of critical theory in adult education (2005) in which he gives a concise description of why the language classroom is an ideal setting for the effective implementation of critical theory:

> Ideologies are hard to detect since they are embedded in language, social habits, and cultural forms that combine to shape the way we think

about the world. They appear as common sense, as givens, rather than as beliefs that are deliberately skewed to support the interests of a powerful minority. (Brookfield, 2005, 41)

In my first-year language classroom, we explore colonialism while learning history, we discuss race and immigration in culture lessons and we work to uncover our own biases, the ideologies that we unknowingly subscribe to because they are embedded in our language and culture. Of course, my students and I are not alone in this critical approach to language learning. Pennycook describes language classrooms as 'sites of cultural struggle, contexts in which different versions of the world are battled over' (2001: 128). In its nature, the language classroom is a place where worlds collide and identities are questioned.

How does critical pedagogy differ from traditional views of educational practices? Pennycook defines classroom practice as a political struggle, advocating 'a view of the classroom as a microcosm of the larger social and cultural world, reflecting, reproducing, and changing that world' (2001: 138). An instructor who employs critical pedagogies in the classroom is doing 'dangerous work' (2001: 138) in part because critical pedagogy resists the primary social purpose of education, which Pennycook describes as the reproduction of cultural and social conditions of a group through the education of the younger members. The purpose of education is to indoctrinate the young with the social ideology that will help them be successful members of their group (Kennedy, 1990). Schools, including colleges and universities, are in their simplest form social institutions that prepare students to function and even thrive in the society in which they live.

To frame the issue in the vocabulary of transformative learning theory, *traditional pedagogy* reinforces the meaning perspective adult students have inherited from their social conditioning. *Critical pedagogy* seeks to transform students' meaning perspective, seeking out the conflict with students' assumptions and interpretations and then engaging in critically reflective classroom activities in order to understand the weight of the conflict. A language educator who employs critical pedagogies in the classroom is engaging in work with the potential to change not just how and what students learn about language but also how students view and interact with the world, their ideas, values and beliefs.

## Identity

Norton's (2013) work on identity and language learners represented a new perspective on the concept when it was originally published in 2000.

The term identity encapsulates self-concept, group membership, race, ethnicity, class, religion, gender, sexual orientation and other descriptors. The idea that learners' identities are multiple and resist dualistic categories has been revolutionary for the field of research on language teaching, dominated for so long by tightly controlled scientific inquiry that left little room for the messiness of human experience. Brought to the forefront of our discussions about language teaching, the concept of identity gives us the vocabulary to describe essential pieces of the language learning puzzle:

> Work on identity offers the field of language learning a comprehensive theory that integrates the individual language learner and the larger social world. Identity theorists question the view that learners can be defined in binary terms as motivated or unmotivated, introverted or extroverted, inhibited or uninhibited, without considering that such affective factors are frequently socially constructed in inequitable relations of power, changing across time and space, and possibly coexisting in contradictory ways within a single individual. A fully developed theory of identity highlights the multiple positions from which language learners can speak, and how sometimes marginalized learners can appropriate more desirable identities with respect to the target language community. (Norton, 2013: Introduction)

Norton's description of learner identity is a reaction to the static, controlled variable of previous positivistic language research. Where past learners were reduced to what Pennycook (2001) termed language-learning machines, identity theory has given learners the freedom to be complex, culturally situated and context dependent.

## Motivation/Investment

The study of motivation in language students in many ways parallels the study of adult learning. In the field of research on motivation, researchers identify two major categories in language learning motivation. First, students may have an instrumental motivation for learning (not to be confused with instrumental learning as described by Mezirow), meaning that the students see learning as a required step in order to achieve a goal. Students in this category are motivated to learn because of what they will get out of the learning, what the learning will help them attain.

In contrast, students may also have an integrative motivation (Gardner, 2001) for language study. In this category, students identify personally with the target culture, feel affection for the target culture or desire to communicate with people from the target culture. This integrative motivation for learning is associated with improved learning outcomes (Ushioda & Dörnyei, 2012). Research has also demonstrated that motivation is a malleable variable (Kozaki & Ross, 2011) and subject to change due to internal and external factors. This is an important note for language teachers: the learning activities we design can have positive or negative effects on motivation and subsequently on student achievement.

In recent research on motivation (Ushioda & Dörnyei, 2012), simplistic, binary views of motivation have been replaced by more complex analyses that see motivation as unstable, and learning as a context-situated process that unfolds in stages. In this framework, which is closely related to Norton's work on identity, students can be better described as invested in learning rather than as motivated:

> The concept of instrumental motivation often presupposes a unitary, fixed, and ahistorical language learner who desires access to material resources that are the privilege of target language speakers. The notion of investment, on the other hand, conceives of the language learner as having a complex identity and multiple desires. The notion presupposes that, when language learners speak, they are not only exchanging information with the target language speakers, but they are constantly organizing and reorganizing a sense of who they are and how they relate to the social world. Thus an investment in the target language is also an investment in a learner's own identity, an identity that is constantly changing across time and space. (Norton & McKinney, 2011: 75)

For the purposes of this study, the concept of investment better reflects the complexities of the students I got to know during my research. However, as a teacher who wants to influence my students to learn more, I often prefer to think of students in terms of motivation. While investment is something that is embedded in a student's very identity, motivation is a learner variable, separate from core values, identities and group memberships. Using a binary conceptual framework of motivation, the process of helping students move from instrumental to integrative motivation seems much more manageable. The investment perspective, however, honors students' core identities and represents the more current approach to the topic of motivation and its relationship to student attitudes, effort and achievement.

Whether the reader sees more value in the concept of motivation or that of investment, the research in this field contributes to the validation and exploration of the questions of why some students seem to want to learn language more than others and how teachers can create optimal environments for learning.

## Intercultural competence

The process of becoming familiar with a new culture and learning to interact with those from other cultures has been theorized in different ways. Acculturation theory makes clear that the process of learning to communicate in another language is intertwined with the process of learning to navigate another culture (Clément, 1986). Stauble (1980) explains that language acquisition is slowed when there is social and psychological distance between the learner and the target language group. So, it follows that if teachers can encourage students to come in closer contact with the target culture, effectively minimizing that social and psychological distance, they can help students learn language. Schumann (1986) created a model for acculturation in language learning that hypothesizes that a greater degree of acculturation provides for a greater degree of language learning. Once again, here we find evidence to support the idea that teachers can best ensure language learning by promoting intercultural proficiency.

Previous research on acculturation as a theoretical model is not directly related to the findings in this study. However, understanding these previous contributions is important for a couple of reasons. First, Schumann's model of acculturation will become a reference point for subsequent scholarly work on acculturation (Citron, 2001), leading to current work on interculturality. Second, this research begins to point teachers toward the idea that culture is not an add-on to language instruction, but rather that culture is a foundational element of language instruction. Teaching culture promotes language acquisition.

While in the past, terms such as acculturation, assimilation and integration have been widely used to describe a language learner's relationship to the target culture, the focus is now on *intercultural competence*. The prevailing wisdom about how we should expect students to engage with other cultures has evolved. The goal is not for students to maintain distance and superiority while examining an exotic foreign culture, nor for students to abandon their own cultural backgrounds, beliefs and values in order to embrace another. Instead, scholars use the term intercultural competence (Byram, 1997; Deardorff, 2006) to describe the process of learning to interact with a new culture without losing one's own cultural foundation. The ability to move among and between cultures is most highly valued.

The historical cautionary tale for teachers trying to teach culture and intercultural competence may be to avoid exoticizing the target culture to make it more palatable or desirable for students (Holliday, 2011; Kubota, 2004). The use of critical pedagogies in culture teaching can transform well-intentioned oversimplification and consumerist treatments of culture. It is possible to teach the target culture in a way that promotes deep learning, and works toward dismantling oppressive power structures within and outside of the classroom. The approach to language teaching that focuses on communication while also fostering critical perspectives and developing intercultural competence is sometimes called 'critical' (Pennycook, 2001). In reality, this kind of teaching is a complex task.

For language teachers, the concept of intercultural competence would be more useful in the classroom if we had a clear picture of how an interculturally competent language learner looks and acts, and how he or she arrived at that state. After all, how are we to develop this quality in our students if we have only vague notions of what it looks like and how it is fostered?

Byram (1997) uses the term intercultural communicative competence to describe a student who is able to speak in the target language in appropriate and meaningful ways that respect the cultural expectations of the listener. I especially like Nguyen and Kellogg's (2010) concise description of an interculturally competent language learner as a speaker of culture. According to Deardorff (2006), a person who will become interculturally competent must possess the requisite attitudes of respect, openness and curiosity. In the course of learning, the individual must acquire knowledge and comprehension including cultural self-awareness, knowledge of the target culture and sociolinguistic awareness. This model for developing intercultural competence has clear implications for the adult language classroom. Teachers can use this model as a guide in designing classroom activities that inspire the requisite attitudes and generate knowledge and comprehension.

The connections to adult learning here are strong. Much research on perspective transformation has involved intercultural learning. Taylor (1994) even discusses the development of intercultural competency as a form of transformative learning. Moeller and Nugent (2014) suggest that intercultural competence is an internal transformation and give examples of teaching practices that may encourage this transformation. The practices mentioned make use of the students' L1 and use problem-posing and questioning to increase awareness of differences. The Council of Europe's (Byram *et al.*, 2002) guide for language teachers uses a question and answer format to directly address teacher concerns. If teachers are willing or able to teach culture in the L1, or if the language learners are at a higher L2 proficiency level, it becomes possible to borrow best practices from other fields that also emphasize intercultural competence, such as multicultural and international education and intercultural communication.

## Conclusion

The traditional and communicative approaches, closely linked to the liberal arts and progressive philosophies of adult education, have dominated the debates about language teaching for several decades. However, something new is brewing in the language classroom. Whether it is called *post-methods* or *critical* or another label, in this new paradigm, language learners are seen as complex social beings, and language classrooms as dynamic sites of cultural struggle where language teachers provide opportunities for students to critically reflect on and experiment with new ways of interacting with the world.

# 4 The Class

A case study requires the researcher to take a holistic view of a single participant or group. In this case, I studied a one-semester class and included the students, teachers, physical space, classroom routines and classroom activities during the semester. With such a complex set of participants and other elements, I was interested in designing a study that would capture the depth of the individuals' experiences, as well as the overall dynamic and processes of the class as a whole. There are many ways to record the events in a classroom. I decided that getting first-hand perspectives of the learning taking place would be my goal. But whose perspectives would I get? While, inevitably, I relied on my own perspective, my own observations of what happened in the classroom, I needed the students themselves to report on their own learning and behaviors to get to the heart of their experiences. I decided that three main data sources would be necessary:

(1) participant observation in the classroom;
(2) student learning journals;
(3) individual interviews with participants.

My belief was that by using multiple data sources to examine the classroom from different angles, I would be better able to determine how, when and for whom learning was taking place.

## The College

I chose a first-semester college Spanish class, Elementary Spanish I, at an urban, Southern, community college which I will refer to as Urban Southern Community College or USCC. The metropolitan area in which this community college is located consists of a county of nearly one million people, of whom more than 450,000 residents, approximately 50.6%, are African American (US Census Bureau, 2011). Nearly 400,000 or 43.4% of the county's residents are white. The community college I chose as the setting for my investigation is a large multi-campus institution which sprawls across the urban center and has campuses in the adjoining suburban and rural communities as well. According to the

National Center for Education Statistics (2011), the demographics of the college differ from the city it serves with Fall 2010 enrollments reporting 62% of the student body as African American and 29% as white. Despite the difference, the college represents a racial cross-section of the community. With 45% of students in the Fall 2009 semester (the most recent time period for which age data were available) over age 25, the college serves a substantial number of adult, non-traditional students. For the purposes of this study, any student over the age of 18 is considered an adult; however, I hoped that by choosing an institution with significant numbers of adults over age 25, I would have a wider age range of potential participants for the study.

## The Students

Thirty students had begun the semester in this Elementary Spanish I class. Of the 22 students still attending the class at the point I began observation, 21 consented to participate. Learning journals were only collected for the 21 participating students and interview participants were chosen from the same group of 21. Two factors, occasional absences and students who stopped attending the course before the end of the semester, reduced the total number of students in the class on any particular day.

### The interview participants

Out of the 21 students in the classroom, I invited 8 to meet me outside of class for one-on-one interviews. Although my only selection criteria was that the interview participants should demonstrate evidence of deep learning, it also happened that the students selected were representative of the population of the class as a whole.

#### *Alexa*

At the time of our interview, Alexa was a 24-year-old criminal justice major. Unmarried with no children, she had previously been enrolled at a major research university located just miles away from the community college where she was taking classes. Because of a tragedy in her family and the strain caused by that event, she had decided to transfer to the community college.

Alexa had attempted to take Elementary Spanish I previously because it was a required course for her major, but was left with negative feelings about the course, the instructor and her ability to be successful. In class, she sat in the front row, was always attentive and focused, and seemed to feel genuine affection and appreciation for the professor. She mentioned several times in her interview how positive her experience taking Spanish with Ms Salazar had been, especially when compared with her previous negative experience at the university level.

Despite her enthusiasm, Alexa withdrew from the course shortly before the end of the semester because she feared her test grades would not be good enough to earn a passing grade. I was not aware during our interview that she would drop the course; she informed me in our follow-up communication via email after the semester had ended.

### Bella

An aspiring dietician who hoped to work in a private practice, Bella did not need Spanish for her degree program, but felt like she needed to take the class in order to become fluent in Spanish.

Single and 20 years old, Bella was a frequent traveler to Miami, Costa Rica and other places all over the world. In fact, she traveled to Costa Rica during her spring break in the semester she participated in this research. She came back from her vacation in Costa Rica convinced that learning Spanish was important and that immersion was the best method for learning. She was considering studying abroad the subsequent fall semester.

### Emily

An 18-year-old recent high school graduate from a local high school, Emily came into class with some background in Spanish study from her high school experience. In addition, Emily had a Mexican brother-in-law.

Emily was taking Spanish in order to fulfill degree requirements, but was an eager learner. She had hopes of one day using the Spanish language in her career as a doctor and continually sought out ways to come in contact with spanish speakers and their culture.

### Jade

As a 29-year-old widowed mother of three boys aged 15, 10 and 6, Jade was facing the challenges of returning to college. Having previously worked in an office setting where she had contact with people from all over the world, she decided to pursue a degree in Broadcast Journalism. Jade intended to become fluent in Spanish, and, over the course of the semester, came to believe that the only way she would truly learn would be to develop relationships and interact with spanish-speaking people.

Jade brought with her previous life experiences and knowledge of African-American history that helped her interpret the material in the Spanish course through multiple lenses. Jade had a positive relationship with the instructor and seemed to admire Ms Salazar greatly.

### Joe

Joe was a 26-year-old hospitality management major who worked as a waiter in a restaurant and intended to go into restaurant management as a career. Spanish was not a degree requirement for Joe. He enrolled in the course because he wanted to learn to communicate with the spanish speakers both in his personal life and in his career. He felt that, in the future, it would be important to know Spanish.

Joe regretted not having more time to devote to the class. Between his fiancé, his two-year-old baby girl, his demanding work schedule and some upheaval in his personal life, Joe rarely found time to keep up with the class requirements. Despite that, Joe maintained that he was committed to learning the language at some point.

### Keisha

A 27-year-old mother of two, Keisha was an LPN (Licensed Practical Nurse) who had gone back to school to become an RN (Registered Nurse). When Keisha talked about her job, she displayed a genuine interest in caring for people and providing for them. On the other hand, she seemed tired, overworked and motivated to change her circumstances.

For the five years that she was in nursing, she worked in a prison facility. One of her favorite parts of this job was getting to work with Spanish-speaking female inmates. Keisha had picked up many Spanish words and phrases working with her immigrant patients at the prison. She enjoyed this informal learning so much, in fact, that she decided to take formal Spanish classes at the college. Spanish was not a requirement for Keisha's degree. It would have been easy for her to avoid language study; however, Keisha saw an immediate application for the language.

### Sandy

A 19-year-old degree-seeking student, Sandy did not need Spanish for her program of studies. Rather, she took the class to get in touch with her ethnic roots. Describing her father as English speaking and Caucasian and her mother and grandmother as Latina spanish speakers, Sandy was interested in connecting with her mom and grandma by learning their native language.

Sandy had taken some foreign language before in high school (French, not Spanish), but had dropped out of high school before graduating. Later, she attended a technical college receiving her high school diploma and becoming a certified nurse's aide. After several months of working in her chosen profession, Sandy decided that her ultimate ambition would require a Bachelor's degree in zoology, so she went back to college. Single with no children, Sandy was a full-time student with her eye on transferring to a four-year school.

*Ten*
Describing himself as 'not the most disciplined' student, Ten was highly intelligent and passionate. He gave the impression of being fiercely individualistic both in his appearance and speech. Ten had fascinating contrasts in his background and interests. He was a pacifist who loved studying military history. He was of mixed Jewish, Caribbean and African-American ethnic heritage, ultimately identifying himself as a Black man, and yet was overcome with anger when immigrants could not speak English. Finally, he was a proficient Spanish student who was in danger of failing first-semester Spanish because he refused to do out-of-class assignments or attend class regularly or punctually.

Ten intended to become a history teacher and needed to take Spanish at the community college before transferring to the local university to continue his studies. Single, 29 years old, and employed part-time, Ten expressed a genuine appreciation and affection for Ms Salazar while also being sharply critical of her methods, class structure and even her accent.

## The Instructors

The instructor of record for this class was Ms Dina Salazar (pseudonym). Ms Salazar, or Miss Dina as many of the students call her, is a US citizen originally from Spain. At the time of data collection, she had lived in the United States for over 10 years, most of that time in the metropolitan area of USCC. Ms Salazar, in addition to being a full-time Spanish instructor, was active in the local Hispanic/Latino community and a vocal advocate for many causes related to social justice. Her educational background included graduate degrees in psychology and education and 18 graduate hours in Spanish.

The reader will notice that, when Ms Salazar is quoted in this study, her English grammar and vocabulary are non-native. Ms Salazar learned English as an adult, and, while she speaks fluently, she has a significant accent and frequently uses vocabulary and grammar structures influenced by her L1, Spanish. During my observations, students did not seem to have trouble understanding her for the most part, although I did note a few times where students asked for clarification. In Chapter 6, I will discuss how students revealed during the one-on-one interviews that Ms Salazar's accent became an important and positive aspect of the course.

When I originally approached Ms Salazar about conducting research in her class, she quickly agreed, but warned me that I would not find her class interesting because she does not care much for questions of pedagogy or discussions of method and does not believe herself to use any particular method. She simply teaches the content designated by the department in the most efficient way she knows. At times, in order to make the class more interesting for herself as an instructor, Ms Salazar discusses the issues that matter most to her, like social justice or film or anthropological distinctions between the culture in her native Spain and the culture in which she now lives. Ms Salazar was energetic in class and had a quick wit. Several students mentioned in interviews that they enjoyed her good humor.

One day, a guest lecturer acted as a substitute. Mr Antonio Pérez (pseudonym) was a full-time visiting professor of Spanish at a local university. Because of his close friendship with Ms Salazar, Mr Pérez had offered to step in and lead a group discussion when Ms Salazar needed to be out of town. Like Ms Salazar, Mr Pérez was also from Spain, had lived for several years in the United States and had a background in psychology and an interest in social justice.

## The Classroom Setting

For the adult learner, a college classroom can be an uncomfortable place. In general, adult students are used to feeling competent and in charge of their lives. However, re-entry into college can cause adult learners to feel a lack of confidence in their abilities (Ross-Gordon, 2003) and inner turmoil (Bauer & Mott, 1990). In addition to the anxiety caused by reentry into college, the foreign language classroom specifically can be a very unsettling place for the adult learner. Learner identity can be challenged (Rossiter, 2007). Adults especially may experience negative feelings when they are unable to rely on their linguistic competence in their native language in order to engage intellectually. The class itself, both the physical space and the culture of the classroom, plays a role in the language learning process for adult learners.

The Elementary Spanish I class met on Tuesdays and Thursdays from 2:10 until 3:40 in the afternoon. In our conversations about the course, the instructor, Ms Salazar, mentioned that this particular group of students tended to be reserved and seem tired. In my own experience as a language instructor, I have witnessed that students tend to be lethargic and laconic after lunch. This especially holds true for adult students, who often begin their days quite early to meet family or work responsibilities. Keeping their energy levels up for an afternoon class can be challenging.

I discovered during my observations that this was, in fact, an accurate description of the class. I noted in my field journal that the students' body language seemed quite relaxed; some were almost asleep and many of them were reclined in their seats. It was not uncommon to find students in the classroom before class time with their eyes closed and heads down on the desk or reclining in their chairs with their feet up on the desks or on other chairs. These behaviors may speak to the comfort level of the students in the classroom or to the afternoon exhaustion that many of the students were fighting through.

The classroom was equipped with two large whiteboards that covered the entire front wall of the classroom and required dry erase markers. Also in the front were a long gray table and wooden lectern for instructor use and a small desk occupied by a computer. Above the whiteboards, a retractable projector screen was mounted. In the middle of the ceiling, a digital projector was mounted. The controls for the projector were wired into the wall next to the computer in the instructor's space up front. Facing the front of the room were 15 long gray tables. Each table fit two students. The classroom space was modern and technologically equipped, but well-worn and entirely gray in color, including the gray carpet and gray cement block walls, which gave the room a cold, institutional feeling. There was no natural light, only overhead fluorescent light.

## Teacher/Student Dynamic

The dynamic in the classroom was characterized by a hierarchical power structure in which Ms Salazar was clearly the dominant figure. To be clear, in no way do I mean to insinuate that the instructor was dictatorial or malevolent in her approach. She was often kind and funny in class, and her students generally seemed to like her. I simply mean that this classroom followed a more traditional approach to teacher and student roles as opposed to the communicative ideal.

As explained in the previous chapter, the traditional approach to foreign language teaching employs a rigid classroom hierarchy where the teacher makes the key decisions about what to learn and when to learn it. In a communicative classroom, the teacher's role is that of a facilitator, and the students maintain autonomy over their own learning process and content. The primary role of the instructor in this ideal communicative classroom is to engage students in the processes of learning by guiding them and giving them feedback. I have never personally observed a classroom where this communicative, completely student-centered ideal has been realized. In every classroom I have ever been in, including my own, the teacher retains a great deal of authority in established learning goals and assessing student progress. Ms Salazar's classroom was no exception. She was clearly the teacher and in authority.

As also discussed in Chapter 3, this type of hierarchical relationship between teacher and students may contribute to adult students' comfort level in the classroom. Although adult learners are said to be self-directed learners who desire autonomy over their own learning, the reality in practice is that adults want to know that their instructor is competent, prepared and professional (Ross-Gordon, 2003). While Ms Salazar's classroom could not be described as learner-centered, she was prepared and seen as a competent professor. The students seemed to genuinely respect and appreciate Ms Salazar, particularly in the interviews, and commented positively on Ms Salazar's humor, willingness to assist students and overall teaching style.

Despite the fact that Ms Salazar was an authoritative figure in the class and seemed to be genuinely liked, student behavior was not always ideal. In general, students sat in passive, receptive positions in class (heads down or staring at the desk or their own laps, arms crossed, leaning back in chairs or forward over desks) with varying degrees of attentiveness. This sort of behavior is to be expected from the perspective of Freire (1970/2000) who warns that 'banking education', in which students are seen as passive receptacles, is the result of a hierarchical power structure. Often, students in the back of the room would engage in low conversation during lectures or large group work. In one case, Ms Salazar called out unresponsive students: 'This is voluntary. It's your choice. You can be bored to death or you can cooperate.' In another instance, when students were talking during a large group activity, she stopped the lecture and said, 'Why are you always talking when someone else is talking? This is very embarrassing!' On another occasion during a lecture, she reprimanded a student by saying, 'This is not time for talking. This is time for listening.' These admonishments did seem to bring the class back into order. I wondered in my field journal if these reprimands were having an effect just on the distracting students, or if the entire class perhaps perceived that all talking was discouraged. In the interviews, two students mentioned that there were several distracting students in class and that they were appreciative of the instructor's efforts to discipline those students.

## Student Performance

The class began as a full class of 30 people. Over the course of the semester, about a third of the students stopped attending. Although these students could not possibly earn a passing grade in the class, they very well may have learned something important during their limited time in the classroom; any amount of exposure to cultural and linguistic differences can be a catalyst for a disorienting dilemma (Mezirow, 1991). Therefore, although several students dropped the course, they were not automatically disqualified from participating in the study. In fact, one of the interview participants, Alexa, did drop the course prior to the end of the term.

Several of the students seemed focused and mature, yet many times, student conversations before, during and after class revealed general disinterest in the course and its content. In one instance in particular around the mid-term, the instructor gave students a take-home test. She allowed them one free class period, on a Tuesday, to work on the take-home test due two days later on the following Thursday. She gave students permission to work in groups and even offered to make herself available in class to help individual students. I wrote down the following conversation between two students in my field notes. I was sitting in the back left corner of the room. The two students were sitting near me, discussing the take-home test due that day, expressing their regret for not having been more active learners.

**Student A**: She even asked us if we wanted to come in and regroup in here on Tuesday.
**Student B**: I wish I had done it, man.
**Student A**: Next time we have one of these tests, we need to meet up.
**Student B**: (reading syllabus now): Did we have workbook, too? Blue pages, too? Man, I didn't do none of that.
**Student A**: I wonder how that's going to affect my grade.
**Student B**: Ah man, I don't even want to think about it.

As it turns out, these types of exchanges between students may have been good predictors of how much of the content and skills students would learn, but not necessarily an indicator of whether deep learning would take place. The second of the two students in the above exchange, a young man named Ten, was later selected as an interview participant and displayed evidence that he had experienced a disorienting dilemma and critical reflection as a result of the class.

I found this apparent contradiction fascinating. How is it possible that students could experience deep shifts in their meaning perspective despite doing poorly in a class or not finishing at all? In our private conferences before and after class meetings, Ms Salazar expressed sadness and frustration at some of the student attitudes. It is easy to see how an instructor could become disheartened with such attitudes in her classroom.

From an adult learning perspective, the students in question seem to have a motivation deficit. Ms Salazar assigned the homework, what the students referred to as the workbook and blue pages, in order to provide her students with opportunities to learn the required content. There was a significant assessment based on this work as well. So, their final grades were partially based on this work. While the students seemed to regret not having done the work, they did not become motivated to complete it even when there were negative consequences for their learning or their grades.

We know that adult students become more internally motivated to learn when the learning activities have a clear relevance to their everyday lives (Knowles *et al.*, 2005). It seems reasonable, therefore, that learning activities that make the real-world relevance explicit would produce a higher level of motivation for students. It is also evident that the workbook and homework did not inspire the kind of motivation the teacher had hoped for.

Students in this class occasionally reported that they did not perform as well as they would have liked. However, based on this research, I have no reason to doubt that for students that fail or drop out, even for students that appear apathetic or oppositional at times, transformative learning may still be possible. As I will explain in Chapter 7, the students who did experience transformative learning had important experiences while in the class that allowed them to overcome their lack of investment in other class activities.

## The Textbook

In many kinds of college courses, the textbook is chosen by the instructor and supports the learning objectives described in the syllabus created by the instructor. In contrast, sequenced general-education courses like Spanish are often planned by departmental committees or course supervisors. At USCC, the course objectives and the textbook are prescribed by the department, meaning the individual instructor plans course activities within specific parameters. In practice, the department's prescription dictated that certain chapters in the textbook should be covered by all instructors, although there were no specific controls in place to ensure compliance. Therefore, in the case described in this study, the textbook became the de facto method for organizing course content. The textbook guided the syllabus and larger curriculum.

All Elementary Spanish students at USCC worked with the same textbook. This text, called *Dos Mundos* (Terrell et al., 2005), was written using the communicative paradigm, meaning that it emphasizes using language to communicate over demonstrating grammatical accuracy. This emphasis is evident in its specific way of dealing with complex grammar concepts. Instead of sprinkling grammar instruction in and amongst the activities in the chapter, the textbook concentrated all of the direct grammar instruction and mechanical grammar practice into blue-colored pages at the end of each chapter. The blue pages contrasted with the white pages of the rest of the text, both in color and overall tone and purpose. While the chapter activities were focused on getting students to work together and explore communicative tasks, the blue pages encourage a more traditional, grammar-translation approach to language learning, gave ample grammar instruction in English, and provided fill-in-the blank, matching and other objective practice questions to aid students in mastering the grammar.

The communicative method in its purest form may not seem to allow for such forays into grammar exercises. However, the authors of the textbook hold the position that grammar is an important touchstone for college students learning language, but class time should not necessarily be used to support grammar instruction (McGraw-Hill, 2006). Therefore, the book is written with these blue pages at the end of every chapter so that students may do the exercises as homework. In an appendix at the end of the textbook, students can find all of the objective answers to the grammar exercises. They received the homework assignment from their instructor, but they were responsible for reading and understanding the grammar instruction in the blue pages, completing the activities and then checking the accuracy of their answers in the appendix in the back of the book. This system of homework assignment encourages students to be self-directed learners (Knowles et al., 2005), taking control of their own learning and responsibility for their own outcomes. By then checking the homework assignments again in class, the instructor reaffirms Ross-Gordon's notion (2003) that many adult students find their desire to be self-directed outweighed by their desire to see the instructor as a competent authority.

Another characteristic of the *Dos Mundos* textbook (Terrell *et al.*, 2005) is the cultural and historical topics in every chapter, with the aim of making students become more aware and more accepting of people, places and ideas different from themselves (Knutson, 2006; Chávez *et al.*, 2003). By including in each chapter several readings presenting diverse cultures and perspectives, the textbook itself could potentially contribute to the students' experiences of perspective transformation.

In an Elementary Spanish classroom, a synthetic syllabus is one in which language is divided into discrete units by parts of speech or by some other linguistic category. These units of language are then grouped together to form lessons. For example, one day, the instructor may present the entire present tense verb system in Spanish, or all masculine nouns ending in –ista. An analytic syllabus, in contrast, does not teach words based on linguistic category, but rather presents the words, phrases and skills that may be required in order to successfully navigate a linguistic context or a specific situation. For example, an analytic syllabus would present words, phrases and skills needed to take a taxi or to bake a loaf of bread. *Dos Mundos* (Terrell *et al.*, 2005) is a textbook that creates a sort of hybrid organization of each chapter. In any given chapter, students are expected to discover the content they require in order to navigate certain situations out of the synthetically organized vocabulary and grammar presented in that chapter. Each chapter presents an unusually long list of vocabulary and grammar organized by categories with the expectation that students will learn what is most useful for their own communication.

Ms Salazar expressed to me that she did not have any particular positive or negative feelings about the textbook chosen by the department. In her view, all textbooks are more or less the same, some a bit better, some a bit worse, but she could make do with whatever she was given.

## Conclusion

In this chapter, I described the setting and participants in this case study. The college (a large urban community college), the classroom and the curriculum were described in detail. Additionally, I introduced the instructors and students. In particular, the reader met Alexa, Bella, Emily, Jade, Joe, Keisha, Sandy and Ten, the eight students who were selected to participate in one-on-one interviews, and began to get a sense of the dynamic within the classroom and with the instructor, Ms Salazar.

# 5 How the Class was Taught

In Chapter 3, I outlined ways that language instruction is related to adult education and development. Then, in Chapter 4, I discussed the details of this classroom environment and participants. In this chapter, I will explore the connections between the instructor and the participants, and how instructional methods played out in this classroom. The reader will learn the specific classroom practices that were most characteristic of this instructor's personal approach.

The choices that an instructor makes about instruction are complex and based on a multitude of factors (Borg, 2003). For example, beliefs and attitudes about language learning affect choices, as do the number of years of teaching and the specific skill or content area in question. My study of this class does not go into depth about why this instructor made the choices she did, but rather explores how these choices were related to the kinds of learning described by students. In fact, Ms Salazar herself was reticent to speculate about her own motivations for any particular methodological approach. As a rule, she wanted students to learn not only some language skills, but even more so, she wanted them to learn about the world and the spanish-speaking people who live in it. Her methods and classroom practices model that primary motivation.

I observed the classroom to gain first-hand knowledge of the methods and practices of the class, but I also relied heavily on learning journals and interviews to collect this data. At the end of each class period, the entire class took five minutes to fill out by hand a form with questions that prompted students to write about what they had learned and how (see the Appendix for an example of a learning journal form distributed to students). The first question on every learning journal entry for the semester was 'What did you learn in class today?' and the second question was 'How did you learn it?' So, students made brief reports of instructional methods in every learning journal entry.

Sometimes, students reported learning in answer to another question on the learning journal and did not specifically report *how* they learned. In all of those cases, the observation data served to fill in the gaps in the reports of instructional methods. For example, Keisha reported learning that it is okay for children in Spain to display aggressive behavior such as biting. Although Keisha did not report in the learning journal how she learned this, the lesson in which that topic was discussed was detailed in the observation data. I was thus able to rely on triangulation between data sets to fill in gaps in learning journal data.

## How Did Students Learn?

No two days in this class were entirely alike, however, after coding the data, certain instructional techniques stood out as being representative of the overall approach. (1) Direct grammar instruction; (2) the use of English (L1) as the primary language of instruction; (3) small-group oral activities; (4) student learning journals; and (5) the frequent inclusion of sidebars about culture and society were the most consistently used techniques. The viewing and discussion of a film, while only done once during the semester, spanned several days of class time and was mentioned by every interview participant as an important instructional technique and so is also included as a significant characteristic. These six categories are explained below to give the reader a picture of the classroom practices most important to this case.

### Direct grammar instruction

The instructor taught each grammar point in class through explicit, deductive grammar instruction in English using the whiteboard to display verb charts, write and diagram examples and to note important points. After hearing the in-class lecture on a grammar point, students were expected to complete the related homework pages on that topic. In the next class period, there were often group activities relating to that grammar. These activities sometimes came from the textbook but were often supplemented by handouts and worksheets created by Ms Salazar.

Following my discussion of the textbook in the previous chapter, I conclude that the instructor in this classroom focused more on the synthetic aspects of the textbook presentation than on the analytic. Ms Salazar spent more time teaching specific grammar and vocabulary categories than on task-based instruction. Tasks seemed to be used primarily as practice activities to support the content taught explicitly by the instructor. Direct grammar instruction is the traditional way of transmitting knowledge from teacher to student in the method characterized by its reliance on deductive grammar, vocabulary and memorization.

In one instance, the instructor was on the second day of direct instruction on the topic of stem-changing verbs, a category of present tense verbs that undergo a patterned change in the verb stem. Ms Salazar began the instruction by asking, 'What are stem-changers, guys?' to which she received no student response. The instructor went on to write on the board and orally explain the definitions of key terms such as 'stem' and 'pronoun' in English, draw the verb charts for several example verbs from this category and give examples of sentences in which the verbs are used. During the 10 to 15 minute lecture, there was very little interaction. Most students were not looking at the front of the room. I wrote in my field notes at this point that I suspected they had tuned out completely. Evidently, my interpretation was wrong. Seconds later, Ms Salazar cracked a joke and the class laughed. Then a student who had appeared inattentive, because he was not looking at the board or taking notes, raised his hand to ask a question about how these verbs contrasted with those they had previously studied. Suddenly there was evidence that, despite appearances, students were paying attention during this direct grammar instruction and at least one student was actively trying to make meaning.

Many of the students in the classroom took advantage of the opportunities to ask questions in English during direct grammar instruction. However, a few did not. In fact, in every class period I observed where direct grammar instruction was used, some students blatantly laid their heads on the desk or did other unrelated activities while the teacher explained the concepts. On one day when students seemed especially unresponsive, the teacher followed her instructions by walking around the room saying, '¡Ándale! ¡Ándale!' (which translates more or less as 'Move it! Move it!' or 'Let's Go! Let's Go!') while clapping her hands. The students seemed amused and perked up noticeably. The instructor often used humor to draw her students' attention or to lighten the mood.

### English as primary

One reason the verb lesson described in the previous section is aligned with the traditional liberal arts approach to language teaching is its use of English as the primary language of instruction. In some foreign language classrooms, students are taught using their native language or L1. In communicative classrooms, students learn the target language by actually hearing and speaking in that language, the L2, with only limited, isolated use of the L1. Using the L2 is intended primarily to promote language acquisition and fluency. However, this poses risks for adult learners.

In general, adult students are used to feeling competent and in charge of their lives. Yet, re-entry into college can cause adult learners to feel a lack of confidence in their abilities (Ross-Gordon, 2003) as well as inner turmoil and disharmony (Bauer & Mott, 1990). Added to their anxiety about college re-entry, the foreign language classroom specifically can be a very unsettling place for the adult learner. As already discussed in Chapter 2, adults may experience negative feelings when they are unable to rely on their linguistic competence in their native language to engage intellectually (Knutson, 2006; Lindberg, 2003; Schulz & Elliott, 2000). This volatile situation may lead to one of several possible outcomes. These feelings may be overwhelming for adult students, causing them to disengage from the learning process or even doubt their ability to learn. In another possible outcome, these experiences become a point of transition for adult students, called a disorienting dilemma, and usher in a process of perspective transformation (Mezirow, 1991) where the adult students begin to question their previous values, beliefs and actions, evaluating and incorporating new perspectives into their own.

In order to promote transformative learning, it is vital that instructors give their adult students the opportunity to reflect, react and collaborate with others to move through this difficult transition period. The traditional approach gives students a space where they can interact in the L1, engaging critically and intellectually with the material. The communicative approach, with its reliance on the L2, runs the risk of alienating and marginalizing adult students who need to use the L1 to cope with the shocking experience of learning a new language and culture.

In the earlier example of grammar instruction in English, I was surprised when students revealed through their laughter and questions that they were, in fact, listening and engaged. I wondered if students in a communicative approach class (where instruction takes place in the L2) would feel as comfortable asking complex questions about grammar or if they would pick up on the humor mentioned off-hand during the lecture.

Later, as I reviewed this in my field notes, I noted that there would seem to be an inevitable give-and-take in course content delivery. If one teaches in the students' native language, their communicative competence does not increase. But there are also compensations when using the L1, such as the improved metalinguistic awareness which allows students to draw comparisons between grammar points or between grammar systems. Because much of the classroom instruction took place in English, the students had ample opportunities to ask about differences that arose between their native language grammar and the grammar presented in the textbook.

## Small-group oral production

While all of the direct instruction took place in English, English was not the only language used in the classroom. The instructor sometimes divided the class into smaller groups for Spanish language practice, usually once per class period, although not every class period. This practice is supported by researchers (e.g. Johnson & Mullins Nelson, 2010; King, 2000; Pilling-Cormick, 1997) who have found small-group collaborative learning to be an important component of adult learning. In these small-group practice sessions, the teacher generally assigned a textbook activity or provided a handout for the students giving them questions to ask, prompts to read or a task to perform. The students would then be charged with using the target language, Spanish, to communicate with their classmates and complete the activity.

For example, in one handout which Ms Salazar had photocopied from the instructor resource manual, eleven Spanish questions were listed, each question with a blank to the right. The questions included verbs and vocabulary from the current unit. The students' job was to ask the questions orally within their small groups and have their classmates sign their names on the blank if they were able to answer the question affirmatively. The instructional objective of the activity was to provide an opportunity for practicing oral production. However, from the students' perspective, they were charged with getting as many affirmative responses, and therefore signatures, as possible.

While students never managed to use the L2 exclusively during my observations, they did exhibit behaviors indicating they were enjoying themselves and learning. I noted in my field journal during one such activity that students were using more Spanish than English and actively trying to negotiate meaning amongst themselves. The small groups often laughed and asked each other follow-up questions in English during the activity indicating their interest in the topics and desire to continue the conversation.

One day, at about the mid-point in the semester, the instructor gave the students a small-group oral production assignment and then left the room for several minutes. The students were productive while the teacher was gone, using the target language, working well in small groups, and continuing with the assignment. I noted in my field journal that some students were so focused on the activity that they did not seem to notice that the teacher had left. One student had a question about the activity while the teacher was out. She resolved the problem before the teacher returned and said that she was proud to have figured it out for herself. It was noteworthy to me that, given the freedom to work or not, use Spanish or not, students continued working on the assignment and used more Spanish than English to communicate.

Students reported the small-group activities were important. In our interview, Bella discussed how the small groups allowed her to personalize her learning, to relate the language to her own life. Alexa also found these activities personally important and discussed the impact that the small-group oral production activities had on her:

> I'm a really in-my-shell kind of person and I think I've come out a little bit more... I'm not really a people person. I mean, I am. I like people. I'm not anti-social. I'm just introverted. And I think the more she points you out and wants you to come on and mingle with the class, then we will ask each other questions in Spanish, it helps you to talk to people because I'm usually the one sitting in the same spot, up front, by the pencil sharpener.

When I followed up by asking what instructional method was the most important in Alexa's learning, she repeated the same idea, 'She makes us talk to each other.'

Clearly, Alexa's discomfort in social situations had to be overcome in order to meet the requirements of the course. In the end, she identified the very activities that made her most uncomfortable as the most important to her learning. While there is no way to be sure until the long process of transformative learning is complete, I suspect that this tension between comfortable introversion and successful communication may have set the stage for a disorienting dilemma for Alexa.

Keisha also described the value of the small-group oral production activities. As a working mom, Keisha found the demands of the class overwhelming and reported that when she got to class, usually after working an eight-hour shift, the small-group work was welcome.

> Nine times out of ten I'm just getting off work, so I'm so tired. [My shift is] eight hours and then I have to go sit in class. You know, some participation, getting up and going around talking to each student. She [the instructor] hasn't been doing it as much. When I have to communicate with them, I learn. Even me, sitting in class with these people. Okay, I know their face, they're in class with me, but who are they? So that was kind of fun. But she hasn't been doing it [small-group oral activities] a lot towards the end. You know, interacting and seeing what the other person knows, that kind of helped since I didn't get a

chance to talk to that many people or have a study group. I didn't want to sit out. I wanted to learn it.

Keisha describes in this passage how the small-group oral activities helped keep her attention after a long work day, increased learning, improved her sense of community with her classmates and helped make up for not having a community of learners to study with outside of class – an impressive list of positive attributes. In her view, Ms Salazar was using this instructional method less often as the semester came to an end, and Keisha felt its absence.

Jade explained the mutual support that came from the group activities:

In class, what was helpful for me was the group activities. We were assigned activities in the book. When I worked by myself, I always got hung up. But when I worked with someone else, the thing that my classmate was hung up on, was the thing that I got very clearly, and vice versa. So, it would always help me to get with someone.

One of the interview participants, Joe, considered that the class was not a priority for him and had little impact on his life. The one instructional method he praised, however, was the small-group oral production. Joe reported that, through these activities, he formed new friendships with classmates, particularly with Jade and Ten, and began to open up on a personal level to his classmates.

## Sidebars

One of the hallmarks of Ms Salazar's teaching style was the practice of inserting anecdotes, personal viewpoints and critical commentary related to society and culture in nearly every lesson. Some students described these inserts as 'tidbits'. I have used the term *sidebars* because of their positioning as interruptions. The sidebars were never the main point of instruction, but rather tangents explored during other kinds of instruction.

In one particular vocabulary/grammar lesson, Ms Salazar taught reflexive verbs describing morning routine activities such as 'levantarse', 'maquillarse' and 'afeitarse' (meaning 'to get up', 'to put on make-up' and 'to shave', respectively). After lecturing, students formed small groups for oral practice. While monitoring progress, Ms Salazar called the students' attention and asked them to think about what they were saying. 'Reflect on gender roles. Do all men shave? Do all women? You say men don't wear make-up? What about a drag queen who is going to work? You would be surprised. Some men wear make-up. I am for it. The world is changing very fast. Get adjusted.' In reaction to the instructor's outburst, students smiled, laughed and made comments to one another. They seemed surprised and amused, a generally positive reaction to her statement.

I should also note here that Ms Salazar's students did not seem offended or shocked by her comment. These exchanges took place in April, so they had already spent most of the semester with her and were familiar with her use of problem-posing (Freire 1970/2000) in order to elicit critical reflection from students. The idea that women wear make-up and men do not is a cultural construct. Unless one has taken a critical stance toward one's own culture, gender roles are one of the many cultural constructs that seem like common sense, the natural order of things. In this short exchange, Ms Salazar used critical pedagogy to problematize students' unquestioning acceptance of the idea that the verb 'to wear make-up' should necessarily have a feminine subject pronoun.

In another lesson about prepositions and places on the college campus, Ms Salazar took a five-minute sidebar to describe the similarities and differences between the university systems in the United States and Spain. Students became so interested in the topic that they asked questions about their own degrees and how long it would take to finish course work in another country. During some free time later in the class period, a group of students in the back of the room continued discussing the pros and cons of the Spanish university system.

In one lesson early in the semester, Ms Salazar taught numbers and how to ask and answer the question, 'What time is it?' In the learning journals for that day, several students cited the Spanish practice of rounding off time as the most important thing they learned in that lesson. This information was not presented in the textbook. Ms Salazar had taken a few minutes during the lecture to explain that, from her Spanish perspective, Americans have an obsession with precisely describing the time. She told the class that in Spain no one would ever say, 'It is 8:59.' A Spanish speaker would simply round up to 9:00. While this is an interesting cultural tidbit, it is striking to me that so many students would remark on this cultural sidebar. As I will discuss below, Ms Salazar's sidebars related to culture and society were frequently mentioned in the learning journals and in the interviews by students in this study.

During the interviews, the sidebars produced some interesting descriptions of the teacher's role as a linguistic and cultural insider. In order to explain students' perceptions of their instructor and her frequent and often personal interjections, I find it useful to describe the teacher as a cultural object (Knutson, 2006). By using herself, her own experiences and her own points of reference to explain linguistic and cultural differences, Ms Salazar turned herself into more than just an ambassador of a language and culture or a conduit of a language and culture: she became the language and culture themselves for her students. Learning about their instructor became inextricable from learning about the target language and culture.

Ten experienced something profound as a result of his teacher's frequent sidebars.

Now, as opposed to getting mad when I hear it [Spanish], I try to, more than anything, pay more attention to it because I kind of want to figure out what they're saying. It's kind of flipped. I don't shun it like I did before. And a lot has to do with her presentation of who she is and how it's being presented to me in a way I'm seeing as a positive thing.

Because Ten was biased against the Spanish language, he had a difficult time keeping his cool with English language learners or with people who spoke with an accent. Ms Salazar had a strong accent and distinctly non-native speech patterns. Yet, after a semester of learning from her, Ten's attitudes about language softened, something he attributes to her frequent sidebars in class. If Ms Salazar is good, then the language and culture that she embodies for him must also be good.

## Student learning journals

When I first approached Ms Salazar about participating in this research, we discussed my idea to track student learning through a daily journal that students would complete and hand in during the last five minutes of each class period. The purpose of the journal was to get an immediate and lasting description from students about what they were learning, how they were learning it and how that learning was affecting them. Ms Salazar decided to implement this technique as part of her regular assessment routine and was willing to give me access to the journals for any student who volunteered to participate in the study.

Keeping a journal or diary has been recognized as an effective tool for promoting critical reflection (Cranton, 2006) in general but also in language learning (Pearson Casanave, 2011). In Kolb's (1984) experiential learning model, the second step is personal reflection. Journaling allows students to engage in personal reflection in a classroom. I had originally conceived the journals as a device to help me collect data for this study. However, because the instructor had students complete the journals every day, this also became an important instructional technique. I was taken aback when an interview participant first mentioned the learning journals as a key instructional method. Of course, I should not have been surprised since, in addition to being a widely used method of investigating foreign language learning (Chaudron, 1988; Nunan, 1992), their usefulness in promoting learning outcomes is well documented.

In several interviews, students referred to things they had written in their learning journals. In my interview with Keisha, I asked her if she had learned anything unexpected in class. Her response was, 'Let me think. There was one. I can't even remember, but I made it a point in my journal.' I had all of her learning journals with me, so I asked if she wanted to look it up. When unable to find the point in her journals, she simply repeated, 'I made it a point to write it at the end in my journal.' Later in the interview when I returned to the question, she again referred me to the journals. I felt as if she valued her written responses above her oral responses.

I began to get the sense that some students saw the learning journals as the authoritative record of their classroom experiences. Students sometimes referred to items written in the journals. Maybe referring to the written record gave credence to their commentary. Or maybe students were helping me make the connections between their statements. For example, Alexa, while trying to explain to me the importance of seeing different ways of life through film said, 'You don't realize what goes on in other places until you see it. When you actually see it, I wrote on one of my journals that we did, when you actually see what goes on, you have more respect for mankind as a whole.' I made a note in my preliminary analysis of the interview data that it seemed as if she were citing having written it down in the journal as proof that her statement was accurate.

Bella also cited herself while talking excitedly about the benefits of learning through experience. 'That's how you learn. That's what I wrote on the little sheet [the journal] yesterday about what could improve this [class]: it's interaction.'

Ten referred to the learning journals in a way that caused me to think about how recording an idea in the learning journal validated it. 'It's definitely opened my eyes. I wrote that on my last journal we turned in.'

I wondered how writing down what they learned had changed things for the interview participants. Would they have been as clear about what they learned if they had not been tracking it all semester? Would there have been space during the course for students to engage in critical reflection and thoughtfully describe their experiences if Ms Salazar had not included journals as part of the daily routine? Of course, there is no way to know for sure, but various student remarks suggest this might well be the case.

In addition to referring to the journal as an authoritative account, Ten interacted with the journal in an unexpected way. For much of the semester, the learning journals included the question, 'Since the last class meeting, did you have any experiences outside of class that related to what we are learning in Spanish class?' Ten offered an interesting reflection:

> I am trying to integrate the things she's teaching. I like how she presents the class and I like those things that we fill out every day that say, 'has anything happened outside of class?' I really like that and just that question. Just being asked that, it makes me want to have an answer. Just the fact that you care or you want to know is any of this shit affecting my life other than just for school and grades. It makes me want to have a good answer for that.

In designing this study, I knew I wanted to get as close as possible to the class and to the students, but without unduly changing the trajectory of the instructional methods or of student learning. On one hand, Ten's response to the learning journals and to one question in particular caused me to focus inward on myself as a researcher and on the study I had designed. This revelation caused me to revisit assumptions I had taken for granted. As a qualitative researcher, introspection and reassessment is clearly a positive thing.

On the other hand, I recognize in Ten's statement that it was not necessarily the journaling that was transformative for him; most important were (a) the perceived interest on the part of his professor, and (b) being held accountable each day for a new answer. From Ten's perspective, Ms Salazar had used the journal to ask him a direct question about how he was interacting with the content, and Ten rose to the occasion.

### Film

Ms Salazar presented the film *In the Time of the Butterflies* in class. Based on the novel of the same name by Julia Álvarez and set in the Dominican Republic in the mid-20th century, the film tells the story of four sisters famous for their revolutionary acts against the corrupt government of dictator Rafael Trujillo. The film is in English, making it accessible for first-semester students linguistically. In addition, several of the lead actors have recognizable names in American pop culture, so the students may have been familiar with Salma Hayek, Marc Anthony or Edward James Olmos prior to watching this film.

The use of film as an authentic text in the communicative foreign language classroom is an established technique. Using pop culture media such as film in adult education encourages critical reflection (Brookfield, 1990; Guy, 2007).

Before viewing the film, students were informed of the assignments they would need to complete in the form of a report on the film. Ms Salazar distributed three handouts related to this report and went over the handouts with the class, reading the page and giving information and explanation in addition to what was written. The first page had two sides. Side A was a detailed list of the requirements for the report. Questions were bullet-pointed for students as writing prompts. These questions were written in the instructor's distinctively fluent yet non-native English as follows:

- What traditions did you observe through the movie? Describe in detail one of them, what they do, why...
- How was the family and Dominican society in the movie? Comment on the structure, behaviors...
- How the main characters change? Why they change? Where events produce those changes?
- Who were the Mirabal sisters ('butterfly')? Personal opinion of them, their ideal and legacy (provide references from books or internet that can support your opinion)
- One thing that you liked about the movie. Why?
- One thing about the movie that you did not like. Why?

Side B of the instruction sheet had a rubric explaining how student grades would be calculated. The second sheet of paper was titled 'Notes Page' and contained questions for students to ask themselves while watching the movie. This page was intended to guide students' viewing and help them take useful notes on the movie.

The third handout was a two-sided page. Side A had an example of an essay written about a different movie that the instructor had deemed a well-written, positive example of student work. Passages were underlined or circled to draw students' attention to especially well-done items. Side B of the same page had what the instructor had deemed a poorly-written report, a negative example of student work. This essay had a handwritten note at the bottom explaining the instructor's assessment of its shortcomings.

All three of the handouts were created by the instructor and explained thoroughly in class. During the explanation of the assignment and corresponding handouts, the instructor described how watching a movie in a college classroom is different from watching a movie for pleasure. Ms

Salazar introduced anthropological and psychological research methods and encouraged students to actively look for important details instead of passively taking in the movie. In addition to introducing research methods, Ms Salazar gave the students civics lessons. At one point she explained how social activists in a democracy can affect the laws of the land and how activists have fewer options in a dictatorship. She described the different branches of government, sources of political power and terms such as 'coup d'état'.

One student asked a question about power in response to this new information. Ms Salazar rephrased the question and repeated it louder for the class. 'How does one person get to have so much power?' To which Ms Salazar shrugged and responded, 'Coup d'état is the official way.' Her matter-of-fact yet subtly critical answer to the student's question is an excellent example of how Ms Salazar used techniques that could be described as critical language pedagogy. Any discussion of inherent power structures falls under the domain of critical pedagogy. The exchange between teacher and student recorded here displays additional characteristics. A coup d'état is obviously a route to power that falls outside of the law and is against the principles of a democratic or peaceful society. By positioning coup d'état as the 'official' route to amassing power in government, Ms Salazar was pushing students to question their previously held beliefs about how governments act and how power is gained.

Students responded enthusiastically during these discussions. In stark contrast to other kinds of class activities, they were attentive, engaged and actively contributing.

The viewing of the film was broken up into three class periods. During the viewing, most students made good use of the 'Notes Page' given to them by their instructor and took notes at intervals throughout the film. Some students were visibly moved by the film, talking back to the screen or shedding tears at the emotional climax. When the movie was stopped so the class could engage in group discussion, the students seemed eager to participate. Some raised their hands, but most just shouted out their responses to the questions asked.

Ms Salazar introduced the film and assignments on the first day and watched the first ten or fifteen minutes of the movie. She was also present for the viewing and discussion on the third day. However, the second day of the film, during which the class watched about 45 minutes of the film and engaged in class discussion, was led by a substitute instructor. Ms Salazar had to be out of class and had arranged for a substitute to conduct class. The substitute, who will be called Mr Pérez for the purposes of this study, was a friend of Ms Salazar and a Spanish instructor at a local university.

Mr Pérez played the movie for approximately 45 minutes and then led a group discussion about the main characters, important plot points and some historical background. Once the class had gone over all of the questions he posed, he took questions from the students.

**Student:** Is this a true story?
**Pérez:** That's a good question. Somebody's asking here if this is based on a true story? (Class erupts into various responses.)
**Class:** 'Yes" 'It has to be a true story.' 'Of course.'
**Pérez:** Ah, I recommend you go to the Internet, your best friend, and look for this last name in combination with the Dominican Republic. Look for the story of the Mirabal sisters.
**Class:** 'Well, then it's gotta be true.' 'Mirabal sisters.' 'Sounds real.'
**Pérez:** I may be lying to you. How do you know I'm not lying? Because I'm a teacher? I'm the boss? Something like that? I would not lie? I have a poker face when I teach, so... Look for the sisters Mirabal and find out! Is it real or not?

This movie is, in fact, based on a novel which is based on a true story. The substitute teacher has an advanced degree in Spanish Literature, so it is reasonable to assume that he knew the story of the Mirabal sisters is historical. Yet, instead of just answering the student's question, Mr Pérez did two things. One, he compelled the students to become more inquisitive and self-directed, to take more responsibility for their learning, a characteristic of adult learners and best practice in the teaching of adults. Two, Mr Pérez used critical language pedagogy to inspire students to think about the nature of truth and authority and the reliability of their available sources of knowledge. This technique is consistent with the pedagogical techniques used by Freire (1970/2000) to open students' eyes to oppression and empower them to action. Despite being the teacher, Mr Pérez proposed that he might be a liar and that students should verify knowledge for themselves. Instead of reproducing the existing power structures, Mr Pérez was encouraging students to see authority figures as fallible and possibly even malicious or deceptive.

Seeking out additional sources of knowledge is not only an aim of critical pedagogy, but also one of Mezirow's (1991) indicators that perspective transformation may be occurring. Therefore, it stands to reason that Mr Pérez's instructions to students may have nudged them down the path of perspective transformation.

Immediately following this exchange, Mr Pérez used the notes he had written on the board during the group discussion to bring students' attention to a sociological issue.

**Mr Pérez**: Another effect you will see more of as the movie advances. (Points out a particular scene described on the board involving a white blonde girl.) That has a name. It is called *whitening*.
**Class**: 'Whitening?' 'Wow!' 'That sounds bad.'
**Mr Pérez**: Not only dictators did that, but for a long time it was an anthropological issue in Latin America. And people would have in their minds that being whiter or lighter would push you to be more successful in life. People would just see that and try to change the reality [to be whiter] and people like Trujillo would try really hard for his whole nation. He was doing it [engaging in the practice of whitening] for the good of the nation. We've heard *that* argument before.

Whitening is the practice of lightening the overall skin tone of an entire population by eliminating dark-skinned people or by introducing more fair-skinned people into the population. This term is often used synonymously with genocide. While not a major theme of the movie, it is nonetheless present and therefore pertinent to a discussion of the historical context (for further discussion, see Metz, 1990). In the next class period when Ms Salazar returned, she discussed this issue again.

So he [Trujillo] was thinking that that was good for his people. The whiter the people he have, more people would invest money to the island and they would be more successful, have better jobs and better opportunities. So, in his mind, what he was doing was right. That [whitening] was a great plan. Over some generations people would become more white and they would have more opportunities.

Notice that both Mr Pérez and Ms Salazar presented the rationale of 'whitening' with a seemingly sympathetic nod to the dictator who believed in the concept. Both instructors indicated that Trujillo believed he was doing the right thing for his country by creating opportunity by any means available to him. This matter-of-fact presentation of the dictator's agenda, coupled with the emotionally powerful film and some raw details about the actual processes used to enforce whitening, provoked a strong response from most students.

In a traditional classroom, the instructor would consciously or unconsciously seek to reinforce existing power structures and ways of seeing the world. Therefore, one would expect to hear in a traditional classroom that foreign dictators are bad and our own government is good. Information about a foreign dictator's crimes against humanity could be used to reinforce a dualistic, good-versus-evil view of the world.

Yet, in the classroom described in this study, the foreign dictator is at once exposed for racism and committing horrific acts of genocide while also being characterized as well-intentioned in seeking economic opportunity. In their commentary, both instructors made clear their horror regarding Trujillo's philosophies and government. Ms Salazar also recognized that Trujillo had a positive working relationship with the United States and Europe. Clearly, both Ms Salazar and Mr Pérez presented a complex perspective on the real people and events featured in the movie.

Learning to see a racist dictator as a complicated mix of positive intentions and negative actions is potentially an important step toward perspective transformation for some students. People who do horrible things are still people. Our own government aligned itself with that dictator. Maybe our own government is not entirely good, either. Chávez et al. (2003) describe the process through which students move as they learn to critically evaluate both themselves and others. This process involves learning to see ourselves and others as complex and to challenge generalizations. For a student in an early, dualistic stage of diversity development, this may require learning to see the other side as not all bad and one's own side as not all good, a more nuanced view of the Other and oneself.

On another occasion, in a discussion of women's roles in society, Mr Pérez corrected a student who had mistakenly identified the setting of the film as contemporary:

> Remember this is 1930s, a long time ago. Which means that things have changed, to today you cannot extract. You look at the Dominican Republic today and I will tell you one thing, it will shock you but the women are more highly educated than men. That changed. That table turned. But the movie is not going to get that far.

This brief discussion of the progress of women's status in the Dominican Republic had a profound effect on at least two of the interview participants who later mentioned this very point during the one-on-one interviews. In the next chapter, I will discuss the impact of the examples I have described here.

## Use of Critical Pedagogy

Ms Salazar's (and Mr Perez's) instructional choices include elements of both traditional and communicative approaches to language teaching. However, taken as a whole, the classroom practices fit well into the philosophical orientation of critical pedagogy. Osborn (2006) associates critical pedagogy with teaching for critical consciousness and social justice. Norton and Toohey (2004) agree, pointing out that 'the ways that social relationships are lived out in language and how issues of power, often obscured in language research and educational practice, are centrally important in developing critical language education pedagogies' (1). Ms Salazar's classroom was a place where students came to learn language, but also found themselves confronting stereotypes and injustices and reevaluating their own culture in light of a new one.

Through the use of frequent sidebars that drew students' attention to key issues, Ms Salazar guided students through the process of questioning their own assumptions about reality inherent in their native language. The use of film and other media in the classroom are also common traits of critical pedagogy, offering examples as subjects for critical reflection. Guy (2007) explains that the use of pop culture such as cinema in the classroom can 'be a vehicle for challenging structured inequalities and social injustices' (15).

Metalinguistic awareness is most commonly associated with the traditional approach to language education. This is likely because the traditional approach uses the students' native language to compare and contrast linguistic structures in great detail. Adult students feel more stable in a classroom when they can intellectually engage with the material, and grammar instruction in the learners' L1 allows adults to do so. In this case, metalinguistic awareness, discussed previously as an element of one's meaning perspective, could also fall into the domain of critical pedagogy (Reagan & Osborn, 2002). If linguistic knowledge is knowledge *of* a language, then metalinguistic awareness is what you know *about* language including topics such as the social context of language use, language ideology and language variety. Ms Salazar repeatedly asked students to take what they were learning and critically reflect on how the new knowledge compared to their existing meaning perspective. This reflection situates an apparently traditional pedagogy in the realm of critical pedagogy.

## Conclusion

In language classrooms, the ideals of teaching methodology give way to the messy reality of language teaching. In this case, the instructor used some communicative techniques and some traditional practices. The hallmarks of this instructor's personal teaching style were direct grammar instruction, L1 use, small-group L2 production, cultural sidebars, student learning journals, a film and the frequent application of critical pedagogy.

# 6 What Students Learned

When we talk about learning a language, what exactly do we mean? Is learning a language the same as learning a grammar system? Is it memorizing vocabulary? Is it learning to communicate in culturally competent ways? Or is it something else? Most of the research conducted in language classrooms is about linguistic outcomes, in other words, dealing with the questions of how much do students know and how well can they produce what they know.

In this study, I asked students what they learned. I allowed them to conceptualize language learning and self-report on their progress. I discovered that students were learning a great deal and were eager to apply what they were learning.

Participant observation, student learning journals and one-on-one interviews were employed to get a broad view of what students experienced in Elementary Spanish I. The learning journals created a trail of evidence of student learning spanning the course of the semester. The two questions that appeared in every journal and provided information about what and how students were learning on a daily basis ('What did you learn in class today?' and 'How did you learn it?') were insufficient in themselves to determine whether deep learning was taking place for two reasons. One, as Säljö (1979) also discovered, most of the learning reported by students was related to content and skills. Two, deep learning unfolds over a long period of time and students may not be aware of their own learning until they reach the end of the process. Therefore, additional questions were asked to identify if students were having experiences in or out of the classroom that pointed to a transformative process.

The additional questions served to paint a picture of how students were interacting with the content on deeper levels. For example, one journal question asked, 'Since the last class meeting, did you have any experiences outside of class that related to what we are learning in Spanish class?' Two other questions ('Is there anything we learned or discussed that caused you to feel excited, shocked, or disturbed?' and 'Is there anything we learned or discussed that caused you to have any strong feelings or reactions?') were intended to find out if students experienced negative feelings or disorientation while learning. Additional questions asked students for opinions on their learning ('Is there any topic or content that you wish the instructor would address more in class?' and 'Other than grammar and vocabulary, what other things have you learned in class so far?') or for the impact of their learning ('Has this class had any impact on your life?'). Student responses to these questions revealed key learning experiences over the course of the semester, documenting events and ideas before students had a chance to forget details.

Later in the semester, during the one-on-one interviews with selected participants, I was able to explore further student ideas about learning and glean more detailed descriptions of what they were learning. Students reported learning which fell into seven categories: (1) learning content, (2) learning skills, (3) personalized or contextualized learning, (4) learning about learning, (5) learning about differences, (6) learning about connections and finally (7) learning to make sense of accents.

## Content

In their learning journals and in our interviews, students frequently noted that they learned discrete units of vocabulary and grammar. For example, one student wrote, 'I learned the months of the year and the seasons'. Another provided a grammatical rule, 'Anything ending in "z" will become plural by dropping "z" and adding "ces".' Other responses of this sort included:

- 'new verbs and conjugations';
- 'joining words like luego';
- 'Numbers 40–69'.

This type of learning could also be described as memorization, whereby information is internalized in order to reproduce it with no contextualization, personalization or critical reflection. It could also be described as banking education (Freire, 1970/2000) or simple acquisition (Säljö, 1979).

## Skills

Also in this category of simple acquisition or lower level learning, students often described communication skills. Communication skills are the skills necessary to blend discrete units of grammar and vocabulary in various contexts in order to communicate with others. This type of learning requires students to apply content knowledge in practice. Like content learning, it requires no critical reflection on the part of the student.

Students gave various examples of communication skills they learned:

- 'I learned how to carefully listen to numbers and translate.'
- 'I learned how to ask someone's age!'
- 'how to conjugate verbs'
- 'I learned how to put sentences together about everyday things and actions.'
- 'To speak more easily in front of people.'

When students conceptualized learning, they reported the simple acquisition of content and skills.

I think it is important to note here that, from a second language acquisition (SLA) perspective, the acquisition content and skills, as I have termed them in this study, would not be so easily reduced to one simple group. The categories that I describe as simple acquisition are the major focus of the field of SLA, a vast and varied field of scholarship using scientific inquiry to work through the details of how and when to teach what in order to produce maximum learning for students.

However, while the acquisition of content and skills is the focus of classroom-oriented research in SLA, adult learning is more interested in student engagement in deeper mental and emotional processes. The learning I looked for in this study would have required students to critically reflect on the content or on the act of learning, to actively experiment with roles and ways of interacting in the world.

My tendency in this analysis to discount certain kinds of learning that are integral to the language classroom may seem counterintuitive from a classroom teacher's perspective, since what we typically assess in language classrooms is precisely the simple acquisition of content and skills. Yet, in adult learning theory, the learning that is most important is not necessarily represented in the objectives on the course syllabus. In fact, while important kinds of adult learning may not be noticed, assessed or rewarded in many language classrooms, they are happening nonetheless.

## Personalized or Contextualized Learning

In a third category of learning reported by students, the content and skills were made even more relevant to each individual's situation through personalization. In other words, students took the grammar, vocabulary and communication skills and applied them to themselves. For example, several students reported learning the content and skills of describing people in the context of describing themselves specifically.

One student, when describing what she learned from a lesson on dates and times, wrote, 'I learned how to say my birthday', a clear example of personalizing the content. On a day when students used questions learned in class during small-group oral practice, several students mentioned that they learned to say what they liked to do or that they learned about their classmates' preferences. In Bella's interview, personalized learning was described as significant:

> I think whenever we had a sheet asking what we did on Friday night or what we like to do, I think that was great because with that I had to actually put my life into it. I had to think about my life and how to convert that into Spanish. I think that was good. Turn my own experiences into Spanish.

While closely related to the acquisition of content and skills, Bella's response here makes it clear that students were required to interact with the material more deeply while engaging in personalized learning.

In other instances, students gave specific examples of what they had learned about contexts or situations which had been used in class activities. For example, in one fun class activity, students filled out a missing persons' report using the grammar and vocabulary they were learning related to description. Several students mentioned in the learning journal for that day that they had learned how to fill out a missing persons' report, something which was obviously not the main point of the lesson, but rather was intended to offer a practical application for the grammar and vocabulary being studied. It was noteworthy how many times students included these kinds of contextualized activities in their reports of what they learned.

## Learning about Learning

The fourth kind of learning that students experienced represented a kind of meta-analysis of their own learning. One day, in response to the journal question 'What did you learn in class today?', Sandy listed some communicative skills and also 'that I need to pay attention'. In addition to learning about Spanish, Sandy had realized some of her own weaknesses as a student. Another day, a student wrote, 'Nothing really stuck in my head today. I'm in quite a bit of shock from all the things I need to learn. I just wish the speed of the class was slower as far as learning goes.' Many students used the learning journal to record that they were learning about their weaknesses as students.

In a few cases, students reported that they were enjoying their learning: 'I have enjoyed learning, regardless of my difficulties.' Students also reported that they were exceeding their own expectations. 'I didn't know I knew that much!'

In the interviews, students continued to express their feelings and discoveries about learning. Keisha powerfully expressed her frustrations.

> I can't handle it. I can't handle it. I mean, I'm taking this class because I want to learn something new. I should have known that, okay, Keisha, it's not going to happen overnight. It's a learning process. But I want to know this stuff now. I need to communicate. I need to communicate. I need to communicate. Right now.

Keisha became so concerned about her difficulties in learning language that she considered dropping the course. These difficulties were especially troubling for Keisha because of her intense desire to communicate with her patients. In fact, she was only taking the course in order to better serve her spanish-speaking patients.

> We get a lot of immigrant people [at the prison where she works as a nurse], immigration. And they probably won't be there long because they're coming over to wait to get back to Mexico or wherever they come from... And they're the funnest people to work with. ... I love when I have new ones come in, especially females, we get a lot of Mexican females, Hispanic females. And we have to deal, you know, it's hard to translate, talk to them. Especially if you don't know Spanish, just a lot of broken words that I've learned just to be able to talk to them. So I took up Spanish [as a college course].

Alexa also came to the realization that learning language was a painful process:

> I wanted to drop it. I did. Because I was doing bad, not good on tests at all. All through the semester, I've wanted to drop. But I was like, no! I can keep going. I can keep going. I can keep going. I think I might be able to make it. Because it's easier to learn, I mean, I know it when I read it! But I guess [my difficulty] it's just because I'm just starting out. I mean I know it [Spanish] when I'm reading it and when I'm writing it and when I'm in class. But when I'm outside trying to talk, I'm like, I don't know what I'm saying!

Keisha and Alexa came to the conclusion that they might have to drop the course because of their difficulties learning to communicate. Other students experienced similar frustrations but arrived at different conclusions, like Jade:

> I kind of feel like, for some reason, I feel like I really won't grasp it [Spanish] the way I expect to get it just from taking the class. I think it would have to come from interacting in a relationship with someone that speaks Spanish more than what you get out of a class… I thought that I would just learn it from taking the class… I just thought that after that first semester I would know how to hold a small conversation … Interaction and speaking. If I was talking to someone and they said things in Spanish and then they turned around and told me what it was, I think I would retain that a whole lot more than just writing it out…

Jade identified the same problem with her learning as Keisha and Alexa: a lack of communicative ability. However, instead of considering dropping the class, Jade formulated a plan of action. She planned to form a relationship with a Spanish-speaker so she could experience the interaction that she was convinced she needed. Keisha and Alexa were dealing with all of the negative emotions inherent in the early stages of perspective transformation. Jade, however, was further along in the process and was developing a plan to acquire new knowledge and skills. Jade continued explaining how the class itself helped her learn how to learn:

> My teacher came in with a CD, and she played a hispanic CD for us. And to this day, it is still in my head. I cannot get the tune out of my head. It's like, 'dadadada, me gustas tú'. We listened to it so long, it was over and over and over. By the time I left out of class, the tune was stuck in my head. When I laid down at night, I was still saying, 'Me gustas tú.' I think that it was those things that helped me come to the realization that it's going to take the interaction to really get this down pat. The films, the music, all those things stick more than what's wrote on the board or the exercises. It's those things. So there's got to be more interaction than just reading the material, doing the work. It doesn't stick like that. It's about songs and films and conversations.

The song that the instructor had played in class that day was 'Me gustas tú' by the Spanish singer Manu Chao. Jade also explained how she was seeking out some real-world language contexts directly tied to her future career plans. Since she was a broadcast journalism major, she watched the news in Spanish.

> They film the news broadcast in Spanish. So I'll watch it and pay attention to see if I can understand. Of course you have the pictures there to help you understand the story, but I'll listen to see if I can understand what exactly are they saying about. Maybe one or two words will jump out that I'll be familiar with that will help me put it together. So, that also makes me feel this is more of an interaction type thing than just writing it out.

Bella agreed that interaction was the key to solving her learning difficulties. 'That's how you learn. That's what I wrote on the little sheet [learning journal] yesterday about what could improve this [class]; it's interaction.'

Sandy came to a conclusion about her own weaknesses as a student while enrolled in Elementary Spanish I. Toward the end of our one-on-one interview, I asked her what she had learned besides the grammar and vocabulary she had already described.

**Sandy:** That if you want to learn a foreign language, you have to study.
**Researcher:** You didn't know that before you took this class?
**Sandy:** Well, I knew you had to study, but I think I like learning in class better than taking it home and learning, way more.
**Researcher:** What is it about the classroom that you find helpful?
**Sandy:** It's more disciplined. Definitely. There's a schedule. No distractions.

Sandy discovered that her own study skills were getting in the way of her learning outside of class while the structure of the classroom promoted learning.

Emily also felt she had experienced difficulty with learning how to learn Spanish but was becoming more optimistic toward the end of the semester. 'It's like the best feeling ever when you can actually kind of understand something. I'm starting to get to that point when you feel like you are starting to see the light. I'm right there.'

## Learning about Differences

The sixth kind of learning that students experienced was revealed when the students' home language and culture were compared and contrasted with the target language and culture. When differences between vocabulary use and grammatical structures are explored by students, metalinguistic awareness increases. Students also reported learning about cultural differences between the home and target cultures. Discovering contrasts between cultures can be a key event which causes students to critically reflect on their own meaning perspective.

During the course of the class, Ms Salazar frequently used English to throw in additional information about the content. Students seemed to love these sidebars (see Chapter 5) and mentioned them in the learning journals. One student summed up her feelings: 'Learning how some things differ positively or negatively in our culture vs. the Spanish culture was interesting.'

Another student was shocked to learn that descriptive adjectives had different connotations in Spanish than they do in English. The instructor, Ms Salazar, discussed in class that while 'silly' and 'hard-working' are seen as positive attributes in the participants' English-speaking community, in Spanish, the terms 'tonto' and 'trabajador' can have negative connotations. 'Silly' may be synonymous with fun or light-hearted in the Southern United States, but in Spanish it can also mean 'irresponsible' or 'stupid'. 'Hard-working' may be a wholly positive characteristic for many English speakers, but in countries where people work to live, being too hard-working, or 'trabajador', may be perceived as negative. Someone who is 'trabajador' may love to work so much that he or she neglects family and friends. Emily wrote in her journal for the day, 'hard working is not really a good thing?!' Bella wrote that day that she was shocked 'that latin americans take being called silly as a *bad* thing.'

Keisha, a mother of two, noted in her journal, 'It's okay for children in Spanish culture to be aggressive – if [they] bite each other it's normal.' This sidebar discussed an aspect of culture that affected Keisha personally. Was Keisha comparing her own experiences in child-raising to the cultural differences explored in class?

Sandy went even deeper in her analysis of these frequent cultural sidebars from the instructor. After the first month of classes, she was feeling overwhelmed by her learning and wrote in her learning journal that she had been shocked to learn 'that I know nothing about the Spanish culture even though my mother is of Spanish heritage.' This statement reveals a conflict for Sandy and was explored further during a one-on-one interview. In fact, the learning journals and interviews were full of examples of contrast statements by students that could potentially have become disorienting dilemmas. The students who participated in interviews were able to describe several such shocking moments over the course of the class.

As already mentioned in Chapter 5, on another day when Ms Salazar was discussing cultural differences in perceptions of time, she explained that spanish-speakers are more likely to round up or down to the nearest quarter hour and that Americans are more likely to give the exact time. Emily wrote in her journal that day, 'Time is rounded! Here, if it's 11:59, it's 11:59! Wow!'

In our one-on-one interview, Emily gave an enthusiastic account of some of the differences she learned about in class.

> Some of the cultural things I found. Like when she told me that they wake up at eight o'clock! Miss Dina [Salazar], in class, she said in Spain they get up at eight o'clock. Because, you know, we're already awake and we rush out and go, 'Hey, get off the road you crazy maniac!' Yeah, we're already working and they're just getting up. How great is that! They round off their money. They round off their money! They don't do what we do, like 1.99. They just round it to two dollars. It's so much easier. You don't need change. Why don't we do that? Let me see, what was my other favorite thing... oh yeah, the thing she told us about the biting. The kids and the biting. About how it's normal. They bite back! I loved them.

One of the most interesting things about Emily's description of her learning is not just that she reported learning about specific differences between the two cultures. Rather, Emily learned about differences and then critically assessed her own culture in light of the new information. When she discussed how money is rounded to the nearest whole number in Spain, she added that the Spanish method is easier and 'Why don't we do that?' This could be described as a critical assessment of sociocultural assumptions, one of the stages of perspective transformation (Mezirow, 1991). It is also clearly consistent with Deardorff's (2006) intercultural competence development model. The student's openness and curiosity is being fed with new knowledge about the target culture.

Bella was also struck by some of the differences Ms Salazar explained out of her personal experience. She laughed as she recalled a particular example:

> When you ask someone [a Spanish-speaker] how they're doing, they say, 'Oh, I'm not doing too good. I have this and that to do.' And she [Ms Salazar] said, 'And then I came to America, and everyone's like, "Oh,

I'm doing great!"' She was like, 'I thought everyone was taking pills or something!' That's what she said! She said, 'Everyone was so happy!' I feel like, just little things like that [are important]. It's true, though, because it's really like that. But I never learned that in any other classes. I mean, nobody else took the time to know the differences and stuff.

Jade gave the same example to explain how she learned about cultural differences by listening to Ms Salazar's examples from her own life.

Sometimes while she was teaching she would just say, 'It's just in our culture!' You know like, she was so right about this, she pinpointed that in the US, when you pass by someone and say, 'Hi! How are you today?' We always say 'Great!' or 'Fine!' or 'Things are great!' Even when things are horrible! We say we're doing good. And she was like, in their culture, they don't say things are great when they're not. So if you say, 'Hola! How is your day?' They would turn around and be blatantly honest! I thought that was so, I thought, 'We DO do that!' And I'm silly. I found myself when I was walking, going to the library, and I spoke to the guy and he said, 'Fine.' And I thought, that's the point she made! I'll bet he's not just fine! That's just how we do.

In this passage, Jade not only demonstrates that she is learning about differences, but by applying what she learned in class to real situations in her life, she also shows evidence of learning from the next category: learning about connections.

## Learning about Connections

In a few cases, students reported learning about similarities between the course content and their own experiences or previous learning. Ten was a student of history, especially Hitler and World War II. After the first day of watching the movie, he wrote that he learned 'that the Dominican Republic & Central & Latin America went through whitening!' Given his interests, Ten was well aware of whitening in other contexts, but in this class made a new connection to the spanish-speaking world. On the last day of the movie he reiterated this connection: 'They were putting people in work camps before Hitler's time.'

Another student, Joe, wrote in the final journal entry that, other than grammar and vocabulary, he learned 'that our languages are not all that different.' Although he specifically wrote the word 'language' here, later, during a one-on-one interview, he indicated that he felt a connection not just to the language but to spanish-speaking people in general.

Alexa made a strong connection while watching the movie: 'I sort of learned a personal lesson about standing up for what I believe in. I know now that people everywhere have suffered greatly.' Alexa connected the suffering in the movie with both her own beliefs and with suffering around the world.

Bella also connected what she learned in class to other experiences in her life:

> In the movie, you saw how they always ate together and the women cleaned and the man provided. And I learned, in Costa Rica, the woman who helped us out, she had a problem the first day because she had to make her husband breakfast, lunch and dinner, because the men do not cook. The women cook for the men. The men do not cook. Like, they won't even eat if they don't cook. That's the extent of the no cooking! And that's totally different because in my family, my dad's the one who cooks.

Here, Bella actually makes two connections. First, she links what she saw of Dominican culture in the movie to what she saw of Costa Rican culture during her travel. Then, she contrasts both experiences with her own life.

Keisha compared her impression of the Mirabal sisters' circumstances with her own.

> The determination, hard will of them [the Mirabal sisters], I didn't know about how back then in the dictatorship you had to do what he [the dictator] says. What he says or you die, you know? Pretty much. Not being able, from a woman's point of view, not being able to do anything I want. Because if I had been alive back then, I would have been dead as soon as I was born. Coming out of my mama's womb, they say don't cry? Waaah, I'm going to cry. You know, that's just the type of person I am.

For many students, the film was an opportunity to connect the examples they saw on the screen with events and people from their own lives.

Previously, I discussed how Jade made connections between the instructor's cultural sidebars and her own life experiences. Jade also made significant connections out of what she viewed and discussed from the film.

> To my surprise, I really enjoyed the film and recommended it to some of my friends, that you guys have to see this. And it was kind of like a cultural shock. I was amazed that there are some things in Latino history that coincide with some of the things that African Americans have faced. It made me look at it like we really have some things in common. I wasn't expecting to get that out of the course, but I am glad that it was introduced.

In one instance, Jade described a scene when the dictator took an inappropriate liking to a young girl.

> When I first watched the film and I was observing General Trujillo, and then, he kind of reminded me. The emotional part was how he had a liking for the young girl at the play when they were performing. And he took her, you know. And that kind of reminded me of personal experiences growing up when you are under the care of an older man, when they take advantage. You know, you're a young girl or whatever. I didn't like that. I mean that was a personal experience for myself and then seeing that in the film, I was like, wow! They were subject to stuff like that too!

Being able to connect her own history of abuse with what she saw in the film allowed Jade to feel a deep connection with women in other cultures who may have had similar experiences. Later, Jade described still further connections between her previous knowledge and what she saw in the film.

> I guess everybody didn't feel the way I felt about the film. But because I have studied my own history and because I have played a lot of characters [in amateur theater] that were significant in the struggle. I got a chance with my church to be over the entire month of Black history and I did some things with my kids. And I was able to put just different things that have happened throughout generations together and to see that we are doing great regardless of what some people still feel or realize. To get an idea of their [Latinos'] struggle, where they came from and how they came to where they are, it brought an appreciation. It made me look at my teacher in a different way. Like, wow. It was amazing. It brought a level of respect for the culture.

When Jade made this connection between her African-American history and Dominican history, she became aware of their shared experiences of struggle. This awareness inspired respect for all Spanish-speakers and their culture.

## Learning to Make Sense of Accents

In the interviews, another kind of learning emerged. Although students had not articulated understanding accents as a category of learning in the learning journals, in the interviews this kind of learning was a recurring theme. The non-native speech patterns and pronunciation of the professor required many of the students to learn how to make sense of accented English.

A sad reality for many college instructors who are non-native speakers of English is that students tend to see them as less competent and less comprehensible, and subsequently rate them lower on course evaluations (Lee & Janda, 2006; Lippi-Green, 1997; McLean, 2007). Adult students seeing an instructor with an accent as fundamentally less competent could be a real barrier to adult learning given that, as research on adult learners tells us (Ross-Gordon, 2003), they may feel a strong need to see their instructor as a competent leader. Despite the high demand for native speakers in language classrooms, this prejudice against foreign speech patterns persists in language classrooms as well.

Obviously, it is neither possible nor desirable to ensure that adult learners only have native English speakers as instructors of other languages. So, how should we deal with bias against accented speech that may be more difficult for some students to understand? The findings of the present study suggest that language classes may have a role to play in broadening students' perspectives on other ways of speaking.

I have detailed in Chapter 5 how the sidebars converted Ms Salazar into an example of the target culture for students to learn from. In this section, I will explore how the sidebars and her other speech in the classroom allowed her to become a linguistic object as well. In other words, she became a living example of the target language for students to examine and learn.

Ten experienced something profound as a result of learning about his teacher:

> Not to hate on Spanish, but I used to get really mad when I'd be driving and I'd see a billboard in Spanish. You know, I worked at the zoo for a while, selling little strollers to the kids, and we would have a day, we called it Mexican Day, and when the kids came in, I'd be talking to the

kids, because the parents don't fucking speak English. And I used to get really annoyed, like when I'd see a commercial in Spanish. You know, last time I checked, this was the United States of America... I used to get really annoyed and think, you are over here. You learn motherfucking English. I don't want to have to learn shit unless I want to. And honestly, just her [Ms Salazar] being as cool as she is has just toned some of that down. I don't have the random anger that I had before... Now, as opposed to getting mad when I hear it [Spanish], I try to, more than anything, pay more attention to it because I kind of want to figure out what they're saying. It's kind of flipped. I don't shun it like I did before. And a lot has to do with her presentation of who she is and how it's being presented to me in a way I'm seeing as a positive thing.

Because Ten was biased against the Spanish language, he had a difficult time keeping his cool with English language learners or with people who spoke with an accent. Ms Salazar had a strong accent and distinctly non-native speech patterns. After a semester in her classes, Ten's attitudes about accents softened. In this excerpt from our interview, he admits his previously held beliefs about his instructor's accent had changed.

This sounds really bad, but I thought that somebody who is teaching in an American school should have English as their first language. I know that sounds ignorant, but with the accent, it's like I have to do a little more work to understand what she says sometimes, when I shouldn't have to. Other than Spanish, which I have to figure out, I also have to play with her English. I've gotten used to it and it's easier than it used to be. And I do like her, so I don't want to hate on her.

Not only was Ten able to describe the difference between his previous and current beliefs about non-native speakers, he was also able to perceive that his current beliefs were better, that he had improved. He told me in our interview that he knew what he was saying sounded 'bad' and 'ignorant'. He obviously felt chastened in his presentation of his previous beliefs. He had experienced a transformation in the way he thought about that difference, and then had reflected on the change sufficiently to realize that his new perspective was superior. He was even able to describe how his experience with Ms Salazar's accent had improved his responses to the Spanish he encountered in his everyday life.

While Ten had by far the strongest reaction to Ms Salazar's non-native English, he was not the only student to mention her accent. Keisha also had a negative reaction. 'Listening to [the instructor], I was like, oh my goodness, and I didn't expect that, you have to pay attention to everything she is saying.' It may seem obvious to a fellow teacher that a student should pay attention to everything being said in class. Yet, for Keisha, the level of attention she had to pay in this class so exceeded what was required in other settings that she was not sure if she would be capable of it.

In contrast, Alexa, Sandy and Emily saw Ms Salazar's accent and pronunciation as a positive quality. Alexa learned best by 'listening to her talk. I learned better how to pronounce the words because she has such an accent that when I leave the class, it's easier to talk. I like to listen to her talk, I love her accent.' To be clear, Alexa implied here that her instructor's accent both in the target language and in English contributed to her learning. Sandy, while also positive about her instructor's accent in English, acknowledged the steep learning curve that she experienced initially.

> Just through when she would say it aloud how it's supposed to be said. I think that helps. Like, I loved that she had an accent, even though the first couple of days everyone was like, oh my gosh! I can't even understand her! I love that part of the class because it kind of says that, this is how you're going to hear it [Spanish] somewhere else, you know?

Emily, too, appreciated the instructor's accent in Spanish.

> Especially her, she has really helped. Because all of the other teachers I've had have been American and spoke Spanish with a very American accent. So that didn't help me at all. When I first saw her and she started speaking. I mean, my other teachers were good and they taught me the grammatical stuff, but with pronunciation, she made a big difference. She did because she actually knew first-hand what she was talking about.

Emily also made connections between her Mexican brother-in-law's accent and her instructor, drawing some conclusions about differences between regions.

> The accents can be different. I know my brother-in-law's accent is quite different from hers [Ms Salazar's]. He comes from Mexico City and she comes from, I think, Spain, and their accents, the way they pronounce things, is very different. I just thought Spanish was all the same.

Bella also noticed differences between her instructor's Spanish accent and the Costa Rican accent she heard during her travels. 'When I was actually in Costa Rica and they were speaking to me, they are so fast and with their accents, you know what I mean? It doesn't even sound like the same thing I'm learning.'

Many adults, in particular adults lacking exposure to other languages and cultures, find it difficult to understand English from other geographical regions or English that is influenced by a speaker's first language. In previous studies (Johnson & Mullins Nelson, 2010), transformative language learning has resulted in students becoming more aware of diversity in the target language and culture. It seems in this class, students learned to understand and appreciate their instructor's non-native English and even began to distinguish between their instructor's speech and other varieties of Spanish. The ability to (1) appreciate varieties of English other than their own and (2) perceive the L2 as having geographical variation are both important steps not only toward linguistic goals but also toward a more mature appreciation of diversity.

## What Students Did Not Know They Learned

As we have seen, when students reported what they learned in the journals, their answers were usually related to content and skills required for communication. On a few occasions, the content and skills were personalized or contextualized, but often they were not. On the days when the film was shown in class, the answers generally conformed to the topics brought up in the film.

In the interviews, however, I wanted to find out what students were learning on deeper levels than just the content and skills of the course. Unfortunately, whenever I mentioned 'learning' in my questions, students continued to focus on content and skills almost exclusively.

**Researcher**: Think back over the semester and tell me what you've learned.
**Joe**:  Well, more than anything, I've really learned how to read. I can pretty much say hello and what my name is. Other than that, whenever I talk to someone who speaks Spanish, I kind of draw a blank. Like, uh, uh, yeah I did take Spanish, but I can't think of anything.
**Researcher**: Okay, you've learned to read, a hello and what my name is, anything else?
**Joe**: No, not really. Not stuff you just go up to a stranger and say. Like, 'Hey, I put on my clothes this morning.'

Joe is saying here that he had, in fact, learned how to say in Spanish, 'I put on my clothes this morning.' Yet, he rejected qualifying this as learning because it was not useful for engaging in conversation with Spanish speakers. I was intrigued by Joe's assessment that he did not really learn because he cannot go up to a stranger and speak in the target language. Keisha expressed the same sentiment about how much she learned. 'It may not be a lot, I may not know how to say a lot, but later I go and I'm like, oh! I could have said this word!' She believed that, because she had not learned how to speak spontaneously in context, she had not learned a lot.

As I sorted through the data from the interviews, I became convinced that there was a fundamental disconnect between my understanding of *learning* Spanish and that of the students. I was sifting through the answers in search of categories of learning that might indicate that students were grappling with social issues, confronting their own biases or assumptions, or making sense of the world in new ways. Meanwhile, the students in this study were stubbornly consistent in their conceptualization of *learning* Spanish as synonymous with *speaking* Spanish.

Another disconnect between my definition of learning and that of the students' was the expected time frame for learning. I have learned more than one language as an adult and have taught languages for most of my career. I understand the incredible investment of time fluency entails. Yet I discovered that the students did not understand the time it would take. Recall Keisha whose primary frustration with Spanish was that she was not able to use it immediately. 'But I want to know this stuff now. I need to communicate. I need to communicate. I need to communicate. Right now.'

Jade also expressed a desire to communicate immediately in Spanish. 'I thought that I would just learn it from taking the class. I just thought that after that first semester I would know how to hold a small conversation, but... oh no, oh no.' Language learning is a slow process, painfully slow for Jade and Keisha.

Like several other students, Bella experienced learning so powerful that she could not resist comparing all of her new learning experiences to the learning she had experienced in Costa Rica. Yet, when I asked Bella what she had learned in her Spanish class, she described her progress in terms of learning to speak. I have pored over her learning journals and interview transcripts and I know that she was also learning about cultural and linguistic differences, about connections between her own life and the target culture and about what it takes to learn a language. Yet, Bella herself did not recognize these experiences as learning. Several times during our interview when I asked her what she had learned from specific classroom activities, she answered me with some variation of the question, 'Do you mean did I learn how to speak?'

## Conclusion

Knowles' model of andragogy (Knowles et al., 2005) describes adults' life-centered orientation to learning. Adult students who have discovered a need in their lives will turn to education to fill that need. A life-centered orientation to learning is consistent with what researchers know about adult student motivations for going to college (Kasworm, 2003). Bella, for example, was generally motivated by future career aspirations, but she was in an Elementary Spanish I class because she had a real-life need to communicate with a group of people. She was counting on this class to help her fill that need. The only learning that registered for her was learning that helped her address her communication needs.

For the students in this study, learning was conceptualized as content and skills that could be reproduced in real-life interactions. Any other sort of learning, no matter how profound, was not generally regarded by the students themselves as learning. However, students learned about connections and differences, engaged in reflection and analysis regarding their own capacity to learn, and even began to make sense of a previously unfamiliar variety of English. As is clear in this chapter, student learning was multidimensional and profound.

# 7 Transformation and Development

In addition to identifying what and how students were learning, the learning journals and interviews provided evidence suggestive of perspective transformation and personal growth and development. In particular, the experiences students reported were consistent with the stages of transformative learning including exploring new sources of knowledge, becoming more self-directed and critically assessing their own language and culture. The eight interview participants were also able to articulate ways that they experienced personal development while enrolled in the course. These examples of personal growth are related to the stages of perspective transformation, but also represent important kinds of learning in and of themselves. In this chapter, I will explore how the theoretical framework of perspective transformation not only helps explain student experiences but also establishes connections to other theoretical perspectives from adult education and second language acquisition.

## Indicators of Perspective Transformation

Based on transformative learning theory, the stages of perspective transformation which I expected to be most likely in the short span of a one-semester class were (1) disorienting dilemma; (2) self-examination associated with negative emotions; and (3) critical assessment of epistemic, sociocultural or psychic assumptions (Mezirow, 1991). The nature of a language course where cultural differences and historical issues were often discussed, and the assumption that language classrooms are fertile grounds for perspective transformation, led me to expect that at least some students would experience one of more of these stages during the semester. I was particularly vigilant for signs that students may have been exploring new sources of knowledge, becoming more self-directed, engaging in critical assessment of their own values and traditions or experiencing strong emotions as a result of their learning, all proposed by Mezirow as indicators of perspective transformation and illustrated in the discussion of learning journal entries which follows.

96  Adult Learning in the Language Classroom

## Exploring New Sources of Knowledge

Mezirow (1991) describes one of the indicators of perspective transformation as 'seeking assistance from a wider variety of sources of knowledge' (193). In the context of a Spanish language class, I interpret this statement to mean that, instead of relying on professors and books, language students undergoing perspective transformation will begin to seek out opportunities to have contact with a wider network of authorities on Spanish language and culture, including native speakers themselves. In addition, becoming more self-directed in their learning would mean a greater frequency of learning experiences outside of the classroom initiated by the student. Therefore, I concluded that students may have been experiencing perspective transformation if they reported repeated efforts to seek contact with the target language and culture.

### Evidence from the learning journals

One of the questions that appeared in every learning journal for the first three months of the semester was, 'Since the last class meeting, did you have any experiences outside of class that related to what we are learning in Spanish class?' Many students used this space to detail chance encounters they had with native spanish speakers. Several mentioned that they were able to understand Spanish conversations they overheard, which was exciting for them. The most interesting entries for this question, however, explained how students had gone out of their way to seek out encounters with Spanish-speaking people. I extrapolated from these encounters that they were both seeking out new sources of knowledge and becoming more self-directed in their learning.

Sandy had consistently written simply, 'No' in answer to this question in her learning journals. Then, about a month into the course, she responded, 'Yes, I bought some pastries at the panaria.' Despite the misspelling here (the term should be 'panadería' meaning bakery), this entry marked a new turn in Sandy's journals. Two weeks later, she reported reaching out to her Spanish-speaking grandmother about the current content: 'I spoke with my grandmother a little about cooking.' After this, her entries became longer and more informative.

Bella made frequent contact with native speakers during the semester. In nearly every learning journal, she reported taking the initiative to make contact with a native speaker. 'YES. I tried to have a conversation with my friend in Spanish, asking her name, where she's from, and how old she is.' Notably, Bella traveled abroad during her spring break and later wrote in her learning journal, 'YES, I've traveled to Costa Rica & the numbers helps with prices.'

Joe mentioned opportunities that arose through his work in a restaurant. Most of these situations occurred spontaneously. For example, Joe waited on customers from Spain or dealt with kitchen staff from Mexico. However, he also demonstrated a desire to initiate contact with these individuals with descriptions of how he used Spanish when he could have used English. 'Yes. Last Sunday I had Spanish (yes from Spain) customers. I had a small "conversation" with them and especially with their 3 year old.' Joe began conducting his normal activities in a new language of his own accord. Early in the semester, he reported that his next-door neighbors were Mexican. Within a few weeks, he had begun speaking to them in Spanish. 'I finally spoke, still very little, with my Mexican neighbors who told me I was good but need practice.'

There was an important distinction in the types of contact students reported. Many, who may or may not have exhibited other signs of transformative learning, reported overhearing native speakers or accidentally making contact with the target culture. For example, one student wrote she 'was driving down the street and saw the sign for "Abuelos",' a Mexican restaurant in the area and also a vocabulary item from the textbook. While interesting to note that the student could understand words in new contexts, these types of chance encounters reveal nothing about whether students are actively seeking out new sources of knowledge. However, Sandy, Bella and Joe, in their statements above, clearly made the effort to initiate contact with the target language and culture outside of the classroom.

One student, Ten, answered simply 'No' for the first month of class when asked if he had any outside contact with spanish speakers. Then, suddenly, he began giving an example in nearly every journal entry of making meaningful contact with the target culture.

## Real-world contact

Lindeman (1961) described one of the fundamental differences between teaching children and teaching adults. 'In teaching children, it may be necessary to anticipate objective experience by uses of imagination, but adult experience is already there waiting to be appropriated. Experience is the adult learner's living textbook' (7). In addition to the experiences students had prior to enrolling in this course, the participants selected for interviews in this study not only brought with them such experiences, but also demonstrated a willingness to extend this experience to communication in real-world settings above and beyond the requirements of the course. Or, to paraphrase Lindeman, they appropriated that living textbook to explore new sources of knowledge about language and culture by accessing native speakers, authentic texts created by and for native speakers and learning contexts where they could access authentic language and culture.

Emily and Bella both indicated that they would like to extend their Spanish study through travel. Emily believed her family connections would provide her with a good opportunity for travel. 'I want to go to Mexico with my sister. She goes to Mexico because he [Emily's brother-in-law] has family there. And maybe I could tag along. I have my passport.' Bella had already started investigating opportunities for formal study abroad. 'I was looking online the other day at a USCC program to Mexico and it's strictly you go there to learn Spanish. So, I was thinking about doing something like that maybe in the fall. I would do the full semester. I really would because you know, I enjoy it.'

Emily also found ways to make contact with native spanish speakers outside of class. 'We had some construction workers come to my job... but I could say "No work tomorrow?" or like "Y'all need anything?" I could communicate with people that I usually wouldn't be able to communicate with.'

Other students found opportunities to practice what they were learning in their daily lives. Ten had contact with a shopper in the supermarket where he worked. In the past, he had avoided these kinds of interactions, but as a result of being in Ms Salazar's Spanish class, he looked for ways to use his Spanish skills in real-life contexts.

> Outside of class, I work in the produce department. And I was able to have a conversation and give directions. I could tell the dude where to find the Swiss chard. Like in Spanish. And I was really fucking proud of that. You know what I mean? I was really excited! That was a really cool experience. When he asked me, my reaction was like, 'Here, I've got a chance! The time is now!' So that was a good experience. My initial reaction wasn't annoyance. It was, let's see how I do here. I am trying to integrate the things she's teaching.

Jade had a real-world intercultural experience when she filed her income taxes.

> Where I went to do my income tax, which really makes me want to learn this thing fluently, there was a Hispanic man who came in, but it was like one family member that could speak very little English. So

she was there representing her family members who were there to file their taxes. And they had a little girl with them and I spoke to her in Spanish and she spoke back to me in Spanish! And then after that the mom assumed that I could talk, so I was like 'No! No! No! I can just say "hello!"' I can speak with the baby! So, that was fun.

The Elementary Spanish class had clearly given this student the confidence to embark on learning outside of the course requirements. Jade was also making plans to engage in social activities that would put her in direct contact with Spanish-speaking people.

So this Saturday, I have a friend that I've been invited out to the [name of dance club deleted]. I like salsa [dancing]! It is so funny because I got to go have free salsa lessons with the salsa dancers. So I learned how to do the dance... So I was excited to have a place to go now.

Several students reported watching TV or movies in Spanish in order to come into closer contact with the language and culture. Emily said, 'I'm watching TV shows. We have this channel. It's channel 15 and it's a Mexico station, actually from Mexico City, I think. They have shows, they have news, and I can understand what's going on.' Jade, a journalism major, also watched Spanish-language television.

So, that particular time I was watching the news in Spanish and they were talking about a house fire and because I knew 'casa', I knew that they were talking about the fire and then 'trabajo' which means work, they were talking about how the firemen worked to put it out. Little things just jumped out to help me make sense of what I was seeing.

Alexa watched movies from Spain and television with Spanish subtitles turned on.

I've watched a lot of Spanish movies! I've watched Pan's Labyrinth and I've watched it over and over and over and after a while, just because you've watched the movie, you're like, I've learned some Spanish now... I saw the Orphanage... I do that with my CSI [the television show], turn it [subtitles] on Spanish.

In the interviews, participants described taking the initiative to interact with the Spanish-speaking world when the opportunity presented itself in real-world encounters. They also described seeking out such encounters and planning trips that would likely result in cultural contact. Through media such as television and movies, students also initiated indirect contact with the target language and culture.

## Becoming More Self-Directed

In addition to exploring new sources of knowledge which resulted in seeking out real-world contact with the language and culture, students displayed signs that they were becoming more self-directed learners, which may indicate the presence of perspective transformation (Mezirow, 1991). A common characteristic of adult learners is the need to be self-directed (Knowles et al., 2005), particularly as they develop higher levels of maturity and personal development (Kegan, 1994). The change that these adult learners underwent as they became more self-directed in their learning can also be described as a change in motivation, another indicator of deep learning and a topic to which I will return below.

### Evidence from the learning journals

Alexa wrote, 'I was intrigued by the movie and looked it up.' This action was recommended by the substitute Mr Pérez during instruction and encouraged by Ms Salazar in her assignments related to the movie. It is important to note that Alexa took these steps and then reported them as a response to her own desire to know more.

Ten and Jade also described pursuing opportunities to advance their learning outside of class, as discussed in the previous section. Ten sought out opportunities in his workplace to practice speaking Spanish. Jade found opportunities in her personal life to socialize with Spanish-speakers.

### Motivation/Investment

Many of these examples of real-world contact with Spanish language and culture are closely related to students' changing motivations or increased investment in language study. Alexa was able to clearly articulate how her motivations had changed.

> Not only after the movie, but way before that, I just thought I'd get credits in Spanish. But then, I actually thought, if I actually learn this, I can communicate with other people! I don't remember when it actually dawned on me, but it just did. Then she makes it seem so

easy the way she just talks Spanish and she's so fun and I'm like, okay, this'll be easy and I will talk to people!

It had never previously occurred to Alexa that she could make real life contact with Spanish speakers as a result of taking this required class. Her initial instrumental motivation for taking Spanish was to get the course credits necessary for graduation. At some point during the semester, Alexa realized that she was no longer there just for the credit; she wanted to learn to communicate and viewed that goal as a possibility.

*Identity and investment*

Jade also reported in her interview how her investment in language learning had deepened over the semester. In her case, this process was tied to her own ethnic and cultural identity and her increased understanding of the connections between her own and the target culture.

Jade's previous work at a bank had put her in contact with international student clients. She described how this professional contact prior to enrolling in the class had presented her with some professional exposure to intercultural communication, leading to her decision to take the class:

> They would sit down at my desk and they would give me more history about what they were studying on America and African-American history and I was like, 'I don't even know that and here I am a Black woman!' It was interesting. So I would sit there and they would share their experiences about what they thought about being here as opposed to where they came from.

This contact piqued Jade's interest in the language, culture and the people. However, it wasn't until she took the Spanish class with Ms Salazar that the instructor's frequent cultural sidebars and the film presented her with more opportunities for transformative learning. When I asked Jade if there was a moment in the semester when she realized that she saw things in a new way, she replied, 'Oh yeah. It was a lot. It was the entire semester. It really was the history. It caught me wide open.'

Jade in particular demonstrates what Norton (2013) terms 'investment'. Jade became progressively more invested in her language study as she realized that her own identities as a woman and an African-American were part of a history that she shared with other Black women across cultural and linguistic boundaries. The more she learned about connections between her own life and the target culture, the more she invested in her learning experience.

## Motivation and effort

As discussed in Chapter 3, instrumental motivation involves students seeing learning as a required step in order to achieve a goal. Integrative motivation (Gardner, 2001), in contrast, in the context of language learning, requires them to identify personally with and feel affection for the target culture or desire to communicate with people from the target culture. This type of motivation is associated with improved student learning outcomes. By the end of the study, it became clear that all of the interview participants had integrative (Gardner, 2001) motivation for pursuing language study, even if at the outset their motivation had been instrumental. However, the relationship between motivation and effort was complex.

Some students, like Bella, began the course with integrative motivation. She described why she enrolled in the course:

> I am taking it because I feel like I will need it. Like when I went to Miami, the loud speaker at Walmart was in Spanish and all the signs, instead of saying 'Men' it said 'Hombres'. So, I feel like it would help, definitely. Anything would benefit. I want to become fluent honestly.

Although she achieved very good grades in the early assessments, it required a real-life experience that demonstrated the immediate value and potential of her knowledge for her to truly apply herself to study.

**Bella:** I'll be honest, the first two tests I didn't study and I passed fine. I can make it through the class without studying and without actually grasping the knowledge. But I learned that I want to retain it and be able to remember it. The first three Spanishes I took I got an A or B in all of them, but I don't really remember much from them.

**Researcher:** How did you come to that conclusion?

**Bella:** I think it was the Costa Rica thing. Just wanting to, when I was there and trying so hard, we did hit a couple of hard points when we were just stuck you know. Neither one of us knew what we were trying to say, and we were just like, ugh, getting out books to find pictures to point at. And I was like, if I actually knew what I was supposed to learn! That's what I was thinking. I could know what I am supposed to say! And that made me want to learn. I should've been paying attention better! I should've studied my vocabulary! It has made me want to take it more seriously. I found myself, even with stuff that we've already taken the test over and I know I'm not going to see it again, just going back and looking over it. Just because if I don't know those small words, how am I going to know anything else.

Bella's motivation, then, began as integrative, but did not result in increased effort to learn until the real world provided her with contexts where she could apply her learning.

Ten also described not needing or wanting to study or complete the course requirements, but demanded a good grade for knowing the content.

I mean, I don't want to denigrate Spanish or anything, but I was like, it's fucking Spanish, man! Spanish One! Like, do I really need to be here all the time? I know what I'm doing. I've still got ten-year-old high school books in my closet. I don't need to be here every day. I don't like her grading system. I mean, if I get a 95% on my test, I want a 95. But you have a homework grade, you have a quiz average, you have a test average. I do my shit and I know what I'm doing when the test day comes, and I don't want to get brought down. On the first one [assessment period] I got a 78%! Because of some workbook and some blue pages. I'm like, dude, that's homework.

Despite the fact that Ten exhibited undeniable signs of transformative learning and changing motivation for learning over the course of the semester, his belief that he shouldn't have to do any homework in order to earn a good grade in the class never changed. His developing integrative motivation never resulted in increased effort in class. In fact, his opinion of the value of the class activities seemed to become more negative as his learning became more evident.

I think that she [Ms Salazar] might misinterpret the sheets that she hands out, you know like those little crossword puzzles that she hands out that you just do in the middle of class for no reason? I think that she might misjudge how much that really helps. You know what I mean? I don't need that. It's just taking up time. I can do this at home or whatever if I need to do this. I don't need it, but I have to just sit there and do it. So that's the only thing, I think some of the time could be spent a little bit better.

*Motivation and achievement*

There is no indication in this study that students necessarily understood the content or got better grades as a result of integrative motivation. Student motivations, then, did not seem to correlate with their performance on course assessments. In Ten's case, increased motivation did not result in a good grade while Bella made good grades even before her motivation increased.

Keisha and Alexa are examples of students who struggled with course content despite their integrative motivation. Keisha, a nurse, had integrative motivation from the beginning. She took Spanish although it was not required and had specific people in mind with whom she wanted to communicate. 'So, when you want to provide the care that they [Spanish speakers] need, accurately, everything they need, I want to be able to communicate with them. So that was my main reason for taking Spanish.' Yet, Keisha threatened to drop out of the class because the material was overwhelmingly challenging for her.

Alexa did, in fact, drop out before the end of the semester because she believed she would fail the course. Significantly, however, she believed the world had opened up to her as a result of the class. She explained what she had come to believe as a result of taking but not finishing the course: 'Well, if you don't know what goes on in other cultures, you're really egocentric. You're really more focused on your own life. You don't realize what goes on in other places until you see it.'

## Critical Self-Assessment

Critical reflection was present in many of the classroom activities the instructor planned for her students. However, when that critical reflection became focused on the cultural and linguistic norms of the speaker's own language, I considered that evidence of critical self-assessment taking place. When students began questioning their own choices, biases and previously held beliefs, they were demonstrating that they were trying to make sense of a disorienting dilemma.

Additionally, this same sort of critical self-assessment is described in the later ethno-relative stages of the diversity development model developed by Chávez *et al.* (2003). Other scholars (Byram, 2008, 2010; Clément, 1986; Citron, 2001; Knutson, 2006; Kramsch, 1993; Mikayla Ortuño, 1991; Taylor, 1994) in foreign language education describe intercultural competence in different ways, many of which could be applied to what the students in this study experienced. Becoming more able to critically self-assess led to an increased openness to another language and culture.

## Evidence from the learning journals

This category of responses was more difficult to identify with confidence in the learning journals. There were occasions when I suspected that students were being critical of their own language, culture, educational system or traditions but it was not possible to confirm that critical assessment was taking place without further information from the student and I determined to follow-up on these responses in later interviews.

Emily wrote 'I found out that cinco de mayo was the day that the US was defeated. I find this odd because in *ALL* the books that I've read, I never heard that before.' One of the reasons Emily has never heard that before may be that it is not an entirely accurate representation of the holiday. ('Cinco de Mayo' means the fifth of May. It is a holiday in Puebla, Mexico celebrating Mexico's victory over the French. The victory at Puebla was a firm rejection of invaders and put an end to US and European expansionism in Mexico. For more background, see Carlson, 1998.)

As I read Emily's statement over and over, I was struck by the implied criticism of her own level of education or perhaps of the books to which she has access. I did not believe Emily questioned the validity of what was taught, since she phrased the US defeat in Mexico as fact, not as her instructor's opinion or as the student's inference, but as a reality. Then, what does she find odd? Is this student saying that her education is lacking? Or is she saying that the books available to her, which apparently are many, have not provided her with all of the information? Is it a criticism of the educational system in which she has been raised? Or of her own lack of exploration? Although I could not be sure, I suspected her self-assessment could be an indicator of the early stages of perspective transformation.

Bella wrote that she had learned that 'a latino will have a more negative attitude + will be real honest vs an American.' While the term 'negative attitude' has a negative connotation, being 'honest' is unambiguously positive. Is Bella saying that spanish speakers are more likely to describe things the way they really are? She is clearly implying that English speakers are not as honest as spanish speakers.

This particular journal entry was written on a day when the instructor was teaching greetings. As part of the lesson, Ms Salazar gave a sidebar talk about the difference between how people answer the question 'How are you?' in different countries. She explained that in her native country, that question elicits a genuine response. If a person asks an acquaintance how she is doing, he should expect a response that reveals her current state, including any complaints she has about her health or other problems. Ms Salazar explained in class that, in her experience in the United States, conversation was always positive and people never admitted when things were going badly, while in Spain and other Spanish-speaking countries, the question 'How are you?' is often met with a truthful response.

For many students in the class, this small difference in conversational patterns was an opportunity to critically reflect on their own culturally determined speech. For example, Jade seemed to have an epiphany about her own language use. She realized 'I always say I'm doing good even when I'm feel [sic] bad.' She was evaluating how she presented herself in light of learning about how spanish speakers present themselves.

## Openness

According to Chávez et al. (2003) the process of individual diversity development includes critical self-assessment at several stages, resulting in an increased openness to other perspectives. This model provides a particularly useful framework for exploring the participant responses in this study since they all began at different points on the diversity development scale and experienced different kinds of progress in their personal journeys.

There is evidence in the Spanish class, for instance, that Ten overcame his own psychological barrier of prejudice. He had exhibited hostility toward the Spanish language prior to taking this class, but, once enrolled, experienced a newfound and unexpected openness.

> So I think, it's definitely opened my eyes... Now, as opposed to getting mad when I hear it [Spanish], I try to, more than anything, pay more attention to it because I kind of want to figure out what they're saying. It's kind of flipped. I don't shun it like I did before.

Ten had even begun to enjoy contact with native spanish speakers, suggesting that he had moved from the Dualistic Awareness stage (Chávez et al., 2003), through Questioning/Self-Exploration and was beginning to show evidence of Risk-Taking/Exploration of Otherness. While he had not reached the final stage of Integration/Validation as outlined in the figure in Chapter 2, by the time of his interview, he was clearly moving in that direction.

Jade also described her newfound openness.

> It was amazing. It brought a level of respect for the culture. It's like a whole 'nother level of respect. Where before I could pass by, and you know, if you don't speak the language, you are not always as courteous or open for conversation. Like we would do when you sit next to someone of the same ethnic group, you know, you can just go chatty-patty. I have

not experienced a lot of relationships or friendships with people of the Hispanic community or Latinos, nothing like that. So, it has me open. That was like a 'Wow!'

Expanding on the possibility of developing new relationships, Jade continued.

My husband passed two years ago, but it made me think, I'm not dating. But I'm like, okay, I could now see myself now dating... It has me open. I'm open, you see. I'm open! That's another thing that shocked me. I could see myself dating outside my race.

Jade had already become aware of cultural and linguistic differences through her life experiences, and, at the time she enrolled in the class in order to explore this new culture, could be described as already having entered the stage of Risk-taking/Exploration of Otherness. As a result of the course, however, she came to see the connection between her own and the target culture leading to her identifying strongly with Hispanic people and validating their language and culture.

Alexa described her new openness as a change in focus. Instead of looking inward at herself, she was looking at the world. 'If you don't know what goes on in other cultures, you're really egocentric. You're really more focused on your own life.' She demonstrated an ability to critically reflect on her own self-centeredness. Later in our conversation, Alexa summed up the result of her learning, 'One thing I've learned, the world is really big.' Alexa had moved from an early stage of unawareness to a place of Questioning/Self-exploration. Bella had a similar reaction while watching the film 'It opened up my eyes to what other people go through.'

## Disorienting Dilemmas

Perspective transformation is a complex process that may take a long time, months or even years, to complete. As unlikely as it is that a researcher could capture the entire process during a one-semester case study, I wanted to at least identify any student progress in this direction. As discussed in Chapter 2, transformative learning theory describes a ten-step process of perspective transformation, the first stage of which is a disorienting dilemma. The disorienting dilemma is the starting point of the learning process. Therefore, identifying how and when these dilemmas took place for the participants in this study was an important first step toward drawing conclusions that may be applicable in other settings.

Seven of the interview participants reported, as a direct result of this class, an experience fitting the description of a disorienting dilemma. These dilemmas were triggered in three ways: by learning about differences, by learning about connections and by learning about learning.

When students learn about differences between the target language and culture and their own, even seemingly minor differences become opportunities to experience disorientation. For example, Emily learned about differences between cultures and, as previously discussed, compared her new knowledge to her own culture. 'They round off their money! They don't do what we do, like 1.99. They just round it to two dollars. It's so much easier... Why don't we do that?'

Jade's story is an example of a disorienting dilemma arising through learning about connections. She experienced a profound dilemma while learning about similarities between her own African-American history and the history of the Dominican Republic. In her words, 'It was kind of like a cultural shock. I was amazed that there are some things in Latino history that coincide with some of the things that African-Americans have faced. It made me look at it like we really have some things in common.'

In Chapter 6, I described in more detail some of the experiences that led to disorienting dilemmas in each of the above categories. In contrast, several students' dilemmas were triggered not by the content, but rather by the uncomfortable experience of learning.

Keisha, a nurse whose motivation for learning was to better communicate with her patients, described her journey.

> It's hard. It is really hard. This has been a tough journey for me, just from January to now. But I mean, it's just hard because everybody [patients] needs care. So when you want to provide the care that they need, accurately, everything they need, I want to be able to communicate with them.

For Keisha, the slow process of learning was the obstacle between her and her goal. Before taking the class, Keisha thought her understanding and using isolated vocabulary words was enough to get by. Now that she has learned grammatical systems, she realizes how hard she will have to work to become fluent.

> I didn't think it would be as hard, because I was feeling okay, I could pretty much just pick [out words] from what I already knew. But it [class] was just a whole different thing. I didn't know it was so much, this has to be with this, this has to be spelled like this, can't use this

with this... I'm just saying a word [at work with patients]... but it's not correct, the whole sentence in general. I didn't think it would be as tough, but it is.

Jade expressed something similar when she said, 'I thought that I would just learn it from taking the class. I just thought that after that first semester I would know how to hold a small conversation, but...oh no, oh no.' Alexa found the class so challenging that she dropped out rather than risk failing.

For several students, the acquisition of content and skills became the barrier that they had to overcome. Reflecting on the process of overcoming that barrier led to even deeper learning about the nature of language and learning. In fact, whether or not the student eventually overcame that initial barrier, reflecting on the barrier had led to deeper learning.

In Bella's case, this reflective learning made her more sympathetic to immigrants who, she came to realize, had to learn English in order to communicate in their new country.

> I feel like Americans are very ignorant. I worked in Myrtle Beach and that's a huge tourist place, huge tourist place. That's all it is. So I worked at restaurants and stuff like that. And when people would come in and speak Spanish, you see the people trying to help them, and they just get so frustrated. They act like they should know what they're saying, and I feel like that is very ignorant. They are from a different country. They don't speak our language. I see what it is to go through to learn Spanish, and I can't imagine what it would be like to learn English. I would have been freaking out! But they were VERY helpful [in Costa Rica] and I don't feel like that's returned when people come here.

Being able to compare and contrast the levels of openness and acceptance of other languages across cultures is an impressive result for a first semester language class. Even during our interview, Bella did not yet demonstrate any understanding of how race, class or economic possibilities may factor into the perceived status of a language or the hospitality toward some groups, despite that being a topic in class at one point.

Like Bella, Emily began to wonder about Spanish speakers' experiences learning English. In particular, she wondered how her instructor had learned English, 'She doesn't talk much about her learning the language itself, but I think that'd be interesting to hear about.' Now that Emily had experienced the difficulty of learning a language, she had developed empathy for and curiosity about others who had successfully completed the process.

Emily also described herself as about to overcome her learning difficulties. 'Because it's like the best feeling ever when you can actually kind of understand something. I'm starting to get to that point when you feel like you are starting to see the light. I'm right there.' She was on the brink of understanding.

A disorienting dilemma may have its roots in classroom practices or other sources (King, 2000; Mezirow, 1991); it may be self-induced, induced by life circumstances or by other people such as teachers or friends. In this study, although the focus is on experiences directly tied to instruction, student experiences outside of the classroom, in several cases, prepared them for or contributed to a disorienting dilemma inside of class. Jade, Bella, Emily, Keisha and Joe had experienced some kind of disorienting dilemma prior to enrolling in the class. Joe, for instance, had experienced transformative learning in his past as a result of contact with spanish speakers. In fact, when I evaluated his learning journals, I had mistakenly believed that his transformative learning was occurring as a result of this course. Upon further investigation, I realized that the extreme demands on Joe's time and attention precluded him from experiencing much of anything in the class. He was behind and disconnected from the content. It may have been his previous transformative experience I was reading in his learning journals.

In some cases, previous learning outside the classroom set the stage for new transformative learning experiences in the classroom. For Keisha, who had already learned to see Spanish as different but equally valid through her work, the disorienting dilemma concerned her own expectations for language learning.

Some students came into the class never having experienced a disorienting dilemma around issues of language and culture. Alexa, Sandy and Ten, in particular, had not previously had the opportunity to critically reflect on the clash of language and culture that language study represents. All three seemed to experience two kinds of disorienting dilemmas: one concerned their own learning, the other the language and culture they were learning. In both cases, the dilemma caused them to critically reflect on their experiences.

Once students experienced a disorienting dilemma, they began a process of making sense of the dilemma through critical reflection both outside of class and through class activities. Some students also began to experiment with new roles, relationships and beliefs based on their disorienting dilemmas. Ten discovered a new relationship with the Spanish language and its speakers and actively experimented with new ways of interacting with the world around him: 'I am trying to integrate the things she's teaching.'

Jade began to explore relationships with people of another ethnicity: 'I have not experienced a lot of relationships or friendships with people of the Hispanic community or Latinos, nothing like that. So, it has me open.'

The classroom provided opportunities for a disorienting dilemma and critical reflection, and the individual students made their own way from this point.

## Transformative Classroom Practices

Because of the non-experimental nature of this inquiry, I can make no definitive claims as to whether the classroom practices reported in this study were responsible for the transformative learning students experienced. However, based on the data collected from the students themselves, several practices were integral to their learning.

Two instructional techniques in particular were closely tied to students' realization of cultural differences and connections: sidebars and the film. The frequent discussions of linguistic and cultural topics caused many students to question how the instructor was different from themselves, how the instructor's language and culture were different from their own, and how language and culture affect the way people see and interact with the world. The film, an emotional portrayal of four sisters who rebelled against a corrupt dictator in the Dominican Republic, enabled students to connect emotionally with events that took place far from their own experiences affecting people different from themselves. These two classroom practices were linked to students' disorienting dilemmas and to the critical reflection and self-assessment that followed.

According to Foster (1997), the most important practices instructors can employ are those that extend language learning beyond just a technical skill or mastery of a set of finite items. Rather, adult learners should find ways to apply their learning in new contexts, taking their language skills into the world. This observation certainly applied to the case study classroom. The film allowed learners to experience a different reality and the classroom provided a safe place for discussing that reality. The instructor's frequent sidebars allowed students engaged in the mastery of technical skills to see the big picture of how those discrete pieces of knowledge connected to larger issues.

Several other classroom practices discussed in Chapter 5 were mentioned in the interviews. Small-group oral activities were used to create opportunities for Spanish language practice in the classroom. Several students discussed the multiple positive effects of this method. First, the small-group activities provided opportunities for interaction in the target language and improved communicative skills. If a goal of language study is communicative competence, then this was the classroom activity that students believed best supported that goal. However, the kind of learning discussed here extends beyond learning to communicate in the target language. The greater benefit of small-group activities is that they provided opportunities for students to get to know each other and build supportive relationships. This group dynamic was linked to students' examination of their own meaning perspectives and realization that other students were negotiating a similar experience, a stage in Mezirow's (1991) description of transformative learning.

Finally, students discussed the learning journals as an important instructional technique. The journals helped students make sense of what they were learning and created daily opportunities for critical reflection.

Although students did not mention the use of English in instruction, it was clear during my observations that conducting portions of the class in English allowed students to be fully intellectually engaged in the lecture and activities. Had the majority of instruction been in the L2, I suspect students would not have been able to comprehend, question, or explore the content in the same way.

Direct grammar instruction, or lecture, was not mentioned by students as contributing to deeper learning when this question was explored in the interviews. In fact, students did not often make connections between grammar instruction and learning of any kind. They seemed much more focused on learning to communicate than on more technical aspects of language structure.

## Conclusion

In this chapter, I have identified three key indicators of perspective transformation in the stories of the study participants: exploring new sources of knowledge, becoming more self-directed, and critically assessing their own language and culture. In both the learning journals and the interviews, these indicators were clearly present for many of the students in the class. Additionally, these indicators of perspective transformation have clear connections to other theoretical frameworks. Students initiated more real world contact with the L2, became more motivated or invested, and developed higher levels of enthnorelativity consistent with diversity development.

In a language classroom, it is customary to assess whether students have memorized vocabulary or verb forms. It is also common to use performance assessment to determine if students have acquired the skills to use that content in simulated contexts. I believe that the development demonstrated by the participants in this study has implications for how teachers monitor and assess learning. It is impossible to know with confidence what happened in these students' hearts and minds over the course of the semester, but there can be little doubt that important growth and development took place based on the data collected. Assessing the deep learning processes associated with adult learning is an endeavor very different from assessing language acquisition, both kinds of assessment are possible in adult language classrooms through reflective journaling or other integrated assessments.

# 8 Applications

Studying a language other than English is a core component of higher and adult education. The vast majority of students who take first year language classes as a degree requirement, however, do not go on to become majors or minors in the language. So, if these students will not achieve fluency after only one semester of study, what is the benefit? Equally important, how can we teach our classes in ways that increase transformative and developmental outcomes in such a short period of time? This study set out to explore how adult learning theory can help language researchers, administrators, supervisors and instructors answer these questions by contextualizing the teaching and learning in one language classroom within the framework of adult learning theory, allowing us to pull out promising instructional strategies and classroom practices.

In this chapter, I will explore some of the applications of this work in research and in language education. First, I will summarize the findings of this study and describe how it continues the work of previous scholarship. Then, I will discuss how the lessons gleaned from this research could influence the language classroom, educational program and policy, and language teacher education.

## Summary of Findings

In this book, I have described the primary characteristics of the instructor's teaching method: direct grammar instruction, English as the primary language of instruction, small-group oral practice, cultural sidebars, student learning journals and the viewing and analyzing of a film. Based on my observation of the classroom, student learning journals and interviews with participants, I concluded that all of these practices except direct grammar instruction contributed in some way to deeper or transformative learning experiences for students.

I also found that certain learning categories were more likely to result in deeper learning experiences. First, learning about connections and learning about differences were frequently cited by students as opportunities for disorienting dilemmas and critical reflection. Second, learning about their own learning was a profound experience for many students in the course who had not previously understood how challenging language study would be. And finally, learning to make sense of their professor's accent both in Spanish and English was an important step for several students who described the teacher herself as an instructional method that engaged them in deeper learning.

In particular, transformative learning theory provided a useful framework for understanding the nature of the learning experiences students reported in addition to providing a map for assessing student progress throughout the learning process. Many students reported exploring new sources of knowledge, becoming more self-directed and engaging in critical self-assessment. These learning processes have previously been identified as indicators of perspective transformation and are closely associated with the concepts of motivation and investment, with seeking out real-world contact with the target language and culture, and with diversity development.

The findings of my research paint a clear picture of the immense value of language study for personal growth and in promoting institutional objectives relating to multiculturalism and diversity. The workforce and the general public require citizens who are capable of meaningful dialogue across cultural and social barriers. The adult development experienced by participants in this study makes a strong case for the important contribution of language study, even at the lowest levels.

## Implications for Research

Based on the findings of this research, it is clear that transformative learning theory holds promise as a way to explore and measure the non-language learning that students experience in the language classroom. This study can act as a bridge between existing transformative learning research and future discussions of transformative language learning.

### Connection to previous studies

Taylor (1997), in his critique of transformative learning theory, gives several examples of how future research could help to strengthen the body of literature. This study responds directly to several of his critiques. First, the tendency of research on perspective transformation to look back on learning from a mature perspective was noted as a deficit in the existing literature. This study collected data as the students were learning and just beginning to make sense of their experiences. Unlike many empirical studies on transformative learning, it attempted to capture students in the act of transformation.

Taylor (1997) also asserts that scholars should describe how to foster transformative learning in the classroom. While no direct causal relationship has been established here, the students themselves have shed light on the methods they felt contributed to their transformative learning. This study helps to fill in the gap that Taylor identified.

Another of Taylor's (1997) concerns is that research designs should incorporate other data collection methods in addition to interviews, specifically mentioning observation and content analysis as possible approaches. This study takes multiple approaches to data collection including those mentioned by Taylor in order to create a comprehensive picture of the classroom practices involved in perspective transformation.

Other studies have examined the classroom practices that contribute to transformative learning in a language classroom, one in an ESL context (King, 2000) and the other, a pilot study for the present research (Johnson & Mullins Nelson, 2010), with students of first year Spanish. However, the research presented here is the only one of the three to use multiple data collection methods to triangulate student reports of classroom practices.

## Recommendations for future research

Future research on classroom practices and perspective transformation in college-level foreign language classes could build on the research presented here in several ways. First, while this research took a snapshot of what occurred within the confines of one semester, a mature, retrospective perspective similar to the bulk of transformative learning research in other fields would be useful in analyzing the long-term effects of learning. The students in this study demonstrated the early stages of perspective transformation and significant personal growth and development, but we do not know whether those early stages ever grew to maturity, whether their perspectives were finally transformed.

In this research, the instructor was not interviewed as a participant, but simply observed. When I spoke with her about the study, it was to understand her methods, not her motivations, cultural perspective or ideas about language teaching and learning. My findings indicate that the framework of the class, and therefore of the teacher who designed the class, had a tremendous impact on the ways students explored content in the classroom. In future research, attention could be paid to investigating the social, psychological and epistemological perspective of the instructor in order to make sense of instructional choices.

Finally, the findings of this study describe only one particular instructor's way of delivering instruction. It would be useful to conduct similar research in a variety of classrooms to compare and contrast findings across methodological approaches, philosophical frameworks and individual differences. Based on this research, previous studies (Johnson & Mullins Nelson, 2010; King, 2010) and my own experiences, I conclude that profound adult learning is prevalent in language classrooms. More studies in a variety of settings would serve to reinforce that assertion.

## Implications for the Classroom

So, how does one case study of one class provide us with new insights about language teaching? What implications does this research hold for language teachers like myself who may want to encourage this kind of learning in their own classrooms? Three specific areas of language teaching practice could draw inspiration from this case study: teaching approach/method, activity design and assessment.

### Teaching approach

In Brown's (2009) research on instructional method preferences of students and teachers, students generally preferred more traditional, grammar-focused methods while teachers preferred methods that were more communicative and real-world oriented. The present study exposes the impact of transformative learning on instructional preferences. Once students in this study experienced transformation, they were more likely to prefer classroom activities rooted in real-world interaction.

There was no indication from the findings that strict adherence to either traditional or communicative methods would produce deep transformative learning. The teaching of culture, often an afterthought in both major traditions of language teaching, comes to the forefront when teaching for transformation. Culture is a rich source of possible disorienting dilemmas, opportunities for critical reflection and intellectual engagement. Language teachers who wish to foster intercultural and cross-disciplinary learning need to employ critical and cross-disciplinary teaching practices.

### Learning activity design

Teachers can usefully apply principles of adult learning theory – experiential learning, critical reflection and transformative learning – to their lesson planning and activity design. Regardless of the methodological orientation of the instructor, adult learning theory can help guide the development of specific classroom activities. Constructing activities reflective of best practice in adult education does not imply that teachers have to change their fundamental beliefs about language or their conviction that a particular approach or methodology is superior. Here we look at some implications for activity design of three main learning models: experiential learning, critical reflection and transformative learning.

*Experiential learning*

Many instructors associate experiential learning with culture learning, field trips, service learning and other real-world or simulation activities. However, even with aspects of language teaching such as grammar instruction, the experiential learning cycle can be employed to increase adult learners' opportunities for critical reflection.

For example, in a communicative classroom a teacher may prepare a small-group discussion task about what students did the previous weekend designed to help them acquire language related to leisure activities, including verbs in the past tense. In a traditional approach classroom covering the same material, students may first learn the same verbs and verb structures, and then examine how they are used in a passage from a text. In either case, Kolb's (1984) experiential learning cycle can be applied to the lesson design. Recall that Kolb's model involves four stages: Concrete Experience (CE), Reflective Observation (RO), Abstract Conceptualization (AC) and finally Active Experimentation (AE). In order to maximize the potential for experiential learning in each activity, a teacher can examine which of the four stages is being adequately addressed and which of the four could be further developed.

In our hypothetical communicative classroom, a structured small-group discussion will undoubtedly encourage L2 acquisition. In terms of the experiential learning cycle, the activity provides students with the opportunity to actively experiment (AE) with language. In order to maximize the potential for adult development, however, students need to progress through the first three stages of the cycle before sitting down with their small group to actively experiment. Perhaps students could watch an authentic video or read an authentic text that includes the key verbs and tenses in the CE stage. Then in RO, the teacher could guide the students in noticing the important forms and asking key questions about the text. In AC, students should connect the new forms to larger theories. In this case that could mean connecting the new forms to conjugation rules or cultural values. This approach of moving from the concrete to the theoretical is often referred to as inductive grammar teaching in language education (see Paesani, 2005 for further explanation and an example of inductive grammar in practice).

The first three stages of the experiential learning cycle are then a prelude for discussion. The initial stages could take the form of a large group activity led by the instructor or individual activities prepared by students as homework prior to coming to class. Applying adult learning theory to lesson planning and activity design implies an expansion of the existing activity but does not take away the individual instructor's autonomy over how to conduct her course.

In the traditional approach scenario where students are examining verb forms and then connecting the forms to a text, it is primarily the order of the activities that could be adjusted to fit the experiential learning cycle. The experiential learning cycle could easily be applied by presenting the text first (CE), asking students to notice important details (RO) and then connecting the forms with rules about conjugations (AC). A follow-up activity that requires students to create language based on what they have experienced in the first three stages would be an ideal AE follow-up activity in the traditional approach. This could take the form of a composition in the target language or a new text that requires students to recognize the forms they have learned in a new setting. The activity could be completed in the subsequent class period or as a homework assignment.

As in the case of the communicative classroom, the instructor who uses a more traditional approach does not have to change the fundamentals of her classroom practice in order to incorporate the concept of experiential learning into the lesson plan. The experiential learning cycle amplifies the existing activity.

In this case study, the instructor promoted intercultural learning using an experiential learning cycle. The CE was a movie that provided students with a window through which to view the culture and history of a Spanish-speaking country. Students were provided with handouts that guided them in making observations and asking and answering key questions (RO). The viewing of the movie was followed by a large-group discussion in which the instructor explained cultural differences and forged clear connections to larger cultural and historical issues (AC). Finally, students wrote an essay (AE) drawing their own conclusions about culture, difference and connections. Although the instructor in this case did not explicitly set out to create a lesson that followed Kolb's (1984) experiential learning cycle, her lesson conformed to the underlying principles and produced a profound impact on her students.

Using the experiential learning cycle as a guide for planning would not detract from the lessons' effectiveness in promoting L2 acquisition. Teachers could retain their methodological preferences in the classroom, whether they prefer to focus on form, communication or intercultural competence. In any case, the reframing of activities allows students more opportunities to make sense of their learning in a way that promotes adult learning and development.

*Critical reflection*

Providing students with opportunities to critically reflect on their learning is key in several important learning models such as transformative learning and critical pedagogy. There are many ways to encourage ongoing critical reflection in the language classroom, including the use of learning journals and the use of the L1 as the language of instruction.

*Learning journals*

Although originally conceived as a way to collect data for this study, over time, learning journals clearly represented a very effective way to monitor student progress, as an ongoing formative assessment. The learning journals were reported by students as being important opportunities to critically reflect on what and how they were learning. In many theories of teaching and learning – experiential learning, transformative learning, critical pedagogy and many models of intercultural competence – without critical reflection, there is no learning. Therefore, providing students with ample opportunities to critically reflect on their learning is vital.

In my analysis of the learning journals in this study, students' comfort level and interaction with the learning journals changed significantly over the course of the semester. In the beginning, answers were often just one word. Occasionally students gave flippant responses to questions about whether they had been shocked or surprised by anything they had learned. However, as students encountered more opportunities for profound learning, their learning journal entries became more enthusiastic and detailed. I began to suspect that the learning journals were a reliable indicator of the degree of investment that students were placing in the class. As students became more invested in learning, their journals mirrored that investment.

For teachers considering incorporating learning journals, this evolution has some interesting implications for wider application. First, teachers do not need to specify how much students should write, leaving them to make their own decisions. Second, the learning journal can be a useful tool to monitor otherwise elusive kinds of adult development related to identity, intercultural competence and metalinguistic awareness.

In the class described in this study, students were asked what they learned, how they learned and if they had any experiences outside of class that related to the class. Other instructors could consider using it as an opportunity to collect other kinds of formative assessment data, such as recollection of content and skills or progress toward intercultural competence goals. A final reflective essay that summarizes and expands on how the learning journals reflect student progress toward course objectives would be a useful summative assessment that also fosters the kind of critical reflection necessary for deeper learning. The learning journal could also be a place where students identify goals or record action steps to be completed before the next class. All of these possibilities could encourage students to be self-directed in their learning.

*L1 in class*

Another way the instructor in this study encouraged students to critically reflect on the content was through the use of English as the primary language in the classroom. Adult learners, used to being competent communicators in their everyday lives, need to be able to express themselves in their native language in order to intellectually connect with the material. It was clear to me through my observations and interviews that students enthusiastically participated in classroom activities and made personal connections to the content when English was the vehicle of instruction.

While research demonstrates that using the target language as the medium of instruction often results in improved language outcomes, there is room to question whether a rigidly communicative approach leaves room for students to do the reflection and exploration necessary to experience transformative learning. For example, in the classroom described in this study, the instructor frequently, in fact almost exclusively, used English to talk about cultural differences, resolve questions and discuss the course content. This English discussion allowed students to dig deeper into cultural differences and understand the deep values behind superficial differences. Is this type of discourse possible in a classroom that uses only the L2?

Discussion in English also turned a moving Hollywood movie into a memorable lesson on culture, history and the struggle for social equality in Latin America. Alexa, who eventually dropped the course, told me in a follow-up email more than a year after the end of the study that the class made a profound impression on her, and she 'never forgot that movie'. The movie is in English, as was all the related discussion.

All language classes have the potential to become sites of cultural collision, safe places for an instructor to guide students through the process of discovery, questioning and exploration that is required for transformative learning. If students are never able to use their native language to navigate that process, then how likely are they to experience a shift in their meaning perspective? How can adult students be expected to make sense of the new world they are discovering as adults when they have only a very small vocabulary in Spanish?

I should interject a few notes here about conducting a language class primarily in the L1. First, as discussed in Chapter 5, there was a significant component of whole-class Spanish discussion and small-group oral practice in Spanish. However, all grammar instruction as well as the sidebars, film and other culture discussions were in English; and several of the key learning experiences reported by participants were activities conducted in English, the students' native language. This finding is not coincidental. The use of English during certain activities lowered their anxiety and allowed them to more fully engage the material.

However, caution is clearly required when deciding what portion of the class period to spend in the students' native language. In Chapter 1, I discussed the idea that 600 hours of instruction are required to reach conversational fluency. These 600 hours include time spent actually engaged in the L2, whether it be in class or at home but not the time discussing the language and culture in the students' native language. Thus, while an hour of class spent in English discussing politics, history or other important topics may yield important progress toward adult learning goals, it will not further the students' communicative proficiency.

If the goal of my classroom is to produce competent communicators, then a majority of the class time should be spent in the L2 working toward that goal. If the goal of my classroom is to encourage adult development and intercultural competence, then L1 may be the best medium of instruction. In reality, both are goals in most classrooms. Therefore, judicious language choice is necessary in order to ensure that students achieve both the L2 contact hours needed for proficiency and the L1 intellectual engagement needed for critical reflection and personal growth.

The debate about what proportions of L1 and L2 are ideal in a language classroom is ongoing (see Chambers, 1991; Cook, 2001; Edstrom, 2006; and Levine, 2003 for more background), each side holding strong feelings and drawing on competing arguments. These debates can be seen as having their roots in the conflict between the liberal arts and progressive models of adult education. If the goal of language instruction aligns with the liberal arts philosophy of education, then the most important components of that instruction will take place in English so that students can develop their intellectual capacity for analysis across languages and even across disciplines. If the goals of language instruction line up with the progressive philosophy of education, as is the case of communicative teaching with its emphasis on immediately applicable skills, then the development of the learner's capacity in the second language will be given priority.

As described in Chapter 3, in a post-methods and pragmatic classroom that does not clearly align itself with either the liberal arts or progressive education, a mix of languages may be required. In my first teaching position as a graduate student teaching assistant, we were expected to speak only in the target language throughout the term, something that worked well in my classroom at the time. Over the years, as I have focused more on intercultural competence and adult development, I have reconsidered this approach and continue to think through the implications of language choice in my classroom. At this point in my own classroom, I employ tools such as journals and online discussion boards that allow students to do thinking and response work in English outside of class, so that we can focus our in-class activities on the L2. This study, like others in recent times (Cook, 2001), supports the careful use of the L1 in the language classroom.

### Transformative learning

Another theory of adult learning and development that has clear applications in the language classroom is transformative learning (Mezirow, 1997). A language class is a space where languages and cultures collide, common sense is called into question and students are asked to perform tasks in a language that feels foreign. These constant collisions may throw students off-balance, momentarily causing them to question the validity of their meaning perspective. Transformative learning theory describes these moments of questioning with the term *disorienting dilemma*. A vigilant language teacher can spot the signs of a disorienting dilemma and plan classroom activities that encourage the critical reflection required to experience transformation. I discussed some of the practical ways critical reflection can be incorporated into the classroom in the previous section.

According to Mezirow's theory, transformative learning does not end with critical reflection. Students experiencing this kind of learning are also likely to discover others who are moving through the same process and validate their own experiences as part of a supportive group. In addition to the benefits for language acquisition, several students noted that the small-group activities allowed them to build relationships with students in the class who were undergoing the same sort of transformation. These small supportive environments were, in all likelihood, important touchstones for students as they negotiated the often disorienting experience of reevaluating their own meaning perspectives.

In addition to critical reflection and finding a group of peers, the transformation process requires learners to explore new possibilities for relationships, roles and actions in the real world rather than in the classroom. In the present study, students were clearly seeking outside experiences in order to try out new ways of interacting with the world. Even in cases where students had not yet formed new relationships, they reported openness to the possibility. Recall Jade, for example, who was open to building friendships and dating with Spanish-speaking people but had not yet had the opportunity. She was, however, actively pursuing opportunities to socialize and become involved in the local Spanish speaking community.

Instructors can encourage adult learners to engage in the transformative learning which leads to greater openness, including contact with speakers of the target language. In the present study, for instance, some students reported that the question in the learning journal that asked if they had any contact with the target language outside of class had inspired them to seek out opportunities. Another route might be to include community interaction as an explicit assessment category. Course credit could be awarded for taking the initiative to make contact with the target language, for example, by participating in community events. Likely, many activities already embedded in language courses, perhaps involving authentic texts or experiences, could easily be adjusted to encourage students to be self-directed in making real-world contact with language.

## Assessment

Two kinds of assessment are found in most classrooms. First, there is the assessment that instructors or institutions plan and implement to document student learning. Assessments may include quizzes, performances and other kinds of formative and summative records of student progress toward learning goals. Although assessment strategies and outcomes vary widely, assessing student learning is a nearly universal component of postsecondary language learning. The other kind of assessment evaluates the performance of the teacher. Administrators, supervisors and governing bodies all have a stake in retaining skilled teachers and identifying room for growth.

### *Student assessment*

Students in this study seemed to believe that language learning primarily consists of being able to reproduce content and skills in spontaneous conversations with native speakers. When this kind of learning was not achieved, they settled for memorizing content in order to reproduce that knowledge on a test. The interviews allowed me to go beyond students' preconceptions and dig into the other kinds of learning. Although students were quite focused on simple acquisition rather than on deep understanding (Säljö, 1979), interviews and learning journals revealed that they had also learned, sometimes incidentally (Marsick & Watkins, 2001), about cultural differences, historical consciousness (Byram & Kramsch, 2008) and other deeper concepts.

Students were not tested on this deeper knowledge as part of their grade assessment and, even at the end of the semester in interviews, tended not to perceive these gains as learning. As Byram (2008) points out, 'What is not tested, is not taught.' The fact that these learning experiences were not explicitly measured in the assessments relates to the course objectives. Ms Salazar taught her course in a way that promoted adult learning goals. However, she did not do so as part of the learning objectives established by her institution which referred only to content and skills related to grammar, culture and communication. Likewise, her assessments reflected the institutional values.

However, what actually happened in her classroom went far beyond the content, skills and cultural knowledge described in the syllabus and the assessments. With the exception of the learning journal, the course assessments failed to capture the profound learning taking place in her classroom. I believe that this underlines the need for more comprehensive and responsive assessment methods in foreign language education. Students are learning much more than linguistic content and that learning should be evaluated formally.

So how can this additional data be feasibly collected? This study gives us a few clues. First, learning journals, as we have seen, can be used as a flexible ongoing method of assessment. In particular, learning journals that include a self-assessment measure could be useful in guiding students toward adult learning goals. Another benefit of self-assessment of this kind is the role it plays in promoting learner autonomy and self-directed learning. Students could be given the responsibility of monitoring their own work and setting goals for improvement.

Second, just as Ms Salazar's students were required to write an essay in English about the historical events that formed the basis of the film they watched in class, the use of English in assessments could provide teachers with an opportunity to evaluate how learners are developing. Requiring students to give complex analyses of cultural phenomena or historical events is not only a good cross-disciplinary assessment measure; it also gives the instructor a window into the internal learning processes of each student. This could be a valuable point of reference during the semester as teachers attempt to track how students are progressing through the different stages of diversity development or intercultural competence.

Finally, despite the fact that many students were engaging in meaningful cultural and linguistic experiences outside of class, these outside experiences did not form part of the course assessments. Teachers interested in promoting adult learning should find a way to track real-world contact with language and culture in order to create a more accurate picture of each learner's progress.

*Teacher assessment*

Evaluation of instructors is also called into question as a result of the present study. While Ms Salazar's students seemed to experience profound, life-changing learning as a result of her instructional methods and reported liking her as a person and instructor, many of the same students complained and were sharply critical of her teaching and assessment methods, even of her personality and speech patterns. On a typical student feedback questionnaire, some of these students probably would not have given Ms Salazar high marks. Considering that neither the students nor the institution developed learning objectives in terms of personal growth and development, it is unlikely that Ms Salazar's efforts in the classroom translated well in student evaluations of her teaching.

Ms Salazar also used a pragmatic approach to methodology resulting in a hodgepodge of techniques and activities designed to move her students toward their learning goals, which is consistent with Kumaravadivelu's (2006) view that, in theory, methodology is clear but, in practice, things get muddy. Had an administrator or researcher observed the classroom only sporadically and without conducting in-depth interviews with students, the methodology may not have seemed aligned with current approaches in foreign language teaching. Clearly, student evaluations and brief, isolated observations are not enough to capture all the strengths of this instructor. It can also be argued that students' unrealistically high goals for conversational proficiency at the beginning of the course, and the fact that they failed to recognize some important aspects of the learning that was taking place, bring into question the usefulness of student evaluations of instructor performance. Can the same students who set unrealistic learning goals evaluate their instructor on whether or not those goals were met?

## In short

Individual teachers interested in promoting deep, transformative adult learning in their classrooms can experiment with some of the activities described in this study. Critical and cross-disciplinary methods should be employed. Classroom activities can be planned with experiential learning, critical reflection and transformative learning models in mind. Approaches to assessment such as learning journals and L1 essays can not only collect data about progress toward adult learning goals but also nudge students toward those goals.

## Implications for Adult Foreign Language Education

One of the premises underlying this research is that postsecondary foreign language study rarely results in communicative competence. However, most research in foreign language education assumes communicative competence as the primary if not exclusive goal of language instruction. My study supports the assertion that additional learning goals are realistic for a first-year language student. Why should adults study languages other than English (LOTE)? Is conversational fluency the only goal? Or is there value in taking just one or two classes? Does the field of language education allow for learning outcomes that fall short of grammatical mastery or communicative proficiency?

The findings of this study suggest that transformative and other kinds of adult learning are possible for students, regardless of whether they continue their language study, or whether they earn a good grade in the course, or even whether they finish the course. In fact, transformative learning seems to produce students who are more open to language and culture and who seek out more real-world contact with language and culture.

### The grading problem

A disorienting dilemma is a learning opportunity for all: you do not have to be a high achieving student to be thrown off-balance. In contrast, students can master all the grammar and vocabulary and be technically proficient, without ever engaging in critical reflection on the course content, on their own meaning perspectives or on how their new found knowledge might impact their lives. Paradoxically, students who earn a perfect score would seem no more likely to experience transformation than those who drop the course before the end. This contradiction is clearly related to the previous discussion about assessment at a classroom level, but also speaks to larger issues about how we conceptualize the value and purpose of the study of LOTE.

In this study, the distinct methods used by the instructor were unified by an overarching theme of critical inquiry and cross-cultural discovery.

Critical reflection and the exploration of differences and connections were clearly highly valued by the instructor, and that value was evident in her classroom. Yet, students' grades reflected the simple acquisition of content and skills, not the core values. It seems that part of the disconnect between theory and practice in the field of foreign language education stems from a grading problem. We advocate for certain kinds of learning without also stressing how that learning connects to teaching and to assessment. I believe an adult learning framework could help reconnect theory and practice on a systemic level. Grades can and should reflect many kinds of learning.

## The value of language study

This book seeks to explore connections between the fields of foreign/second language teaching and adult learning theory, an interdisciplinary approach that serves as a framework for understanding teaching methods that promote the deeper, more critical language learning advocated by scholars and professional organizations. The findings reinforce the value of beginning language courses, even for those who do not go on to higher levels.

As discussed in Chapter 1, a shockingly low number of postsecondary students study languages as part of their degree programs. For example, one survey of foreign language enrollments in the United States (Furman et al., 2007) has reported that just 8.6% of postsecondary enrollments were in foreign language courses. Given the potential contribution that language study makes to critical thinking, intercultural competence, diversity development and other vital areas of adult development, it is perhaps surprising that any university would allow students to graduate without studying a language. Similarly, with such dramatic outcomes in adult development, it is disappointing that so few corporations, governments and community groups provide language instruction to their employees and members.

Of the 8.6% of US college enrollments in languages, only 1.4% were for advanced courses. The large majority of the students studying foreign language in American postsecondary institutions are thus taking elementary and intermediate language courses, usually to fulfill degree requirements. Given the number of hours required to become proficient, it is clear that students who fulfill only a two- or four-semester requirement are not attaining linguistic proficiency. They may, however, be achieving equally important learning outcomes, such as beginning to overcome prejudice, connecting with people very different from themselves and experimenting with new roles and perspectives.

Such outcomes are not often discussed in our larger national and international conversations about language study. Just like the students in this study, when we think about studying a language, most of us imagine the goal to be conversational fluency. However, if we expand this goal to include critical consciousness, historical awareness and openness to difference, the value of a one- or two-term language requirement is clear.

According to the Modern Language Association (MLA, 2007) the goal of the language major should be, 'to produce a specific outcome: educated speakers who have deep translingual and transcultural competence.' The present study suggests that translingual and transcultural competence is an accessible goal for students at the earliest levels of language study and not an outcome reserved just for majors or long-term language students.

## Implications for language instructor training

At a time when scholars are calling for better preparation for language instructors (Johnson, 2006; MLA, 2014), the findings of this research offer useful directions for discussions of the skills future language teachers will need. In many cases, language instructors receive very little teaching preparation. College level language teachers often train for their teaching jobs in MA and PhD programs focused on research or upper-level teaching. Most graduate students who will go on to teach LOTE at the college level spend their time in graduate school learning skills for research or literary criticism. Even in cases where graduate students receive adequate pedagogical training and support, the processes of adult learning are rarely included in methods courses or pedagogy workshops. However, an understanding of adult learning could prove indispensable for teachers navigating their students' complex and dynamic reactions to language learning.

During formal training for their future profession, whether in graduate school or other settings, adult foreign language educators should develop an understanding of adult learning processes in order to nurture deeper learning experiences. The ability to both identify the indicators of perspective transformation and incorporate the classroom practices associated with this transformation will allow a language instructor to expand learning objectives to include critical awareness and intercultural competence. An instructor who is familiar with the processes of adult learning can better create an environment where the stages of adult learning are supported, validated and encouraged.

## Final Thoughts

This research brings to light new findings related to how students learn important lessons about the nature of difference, of connectedness and of learning itself. Several students in this study overcame bias and social division to connect with people who seemed very different from them. Many instructors, myself included, wonder how to teach language in such a way as to improve the world around them, encourage students on their journeys of personal growth, effect social change and inspire students to action. By applying adult learning theory to our classroom practice, we can foster deep transformative learning so that students transform their perceptions of and interactions with the world.

# Appendix

Nombre: _____

Fecha: <u>el</u>　　　　<u>de marzo 2009</u>

## Reflective Journal

Your reflective journaling is meant to capture your ideas, reactions, and reflections as you move through this class. Please feel free to respond openly to the questions. Since there are no right or wrong answers in reflective journaling, you will not be graded on the content of your answer. It is just important that you engage in the act of reflection and record your thoughts here. If you need more room, you may use the back of this sheet of paper.

(1) What did you learn in class today?

(2) How did you learn it?

(3) Since the last class meeting, did you have any experiences outside of class that related to what we are learning in Spanish class?

(4) Is there anything we learned or discussed that caused you to feel excited, shocked, or disturbed? If nothing, then leave this question blank. If so, please explain.

# References

Abrams, Z., Byrd, D., Boovy, B., and Mohring, A. (2006) Culture portfolios revisited: Feedback from students and instructors. *Die Unterrichtspraxis* 39 (1–2), 80.
American Council for the Teaching of Foreign Languages [ACTFL]. (n.d.) Standards for Foreign Language Learning: Preparing for the 21st Century. See http://www.actfl.org/files/public/StandardsforFLLexecsumm_rev.pdf
American Council for the Teaching of Foreign Languages [ACTFL]. (2012) ACTFL Proficiency Guidelines 2012. See http://www.actfl.org/publications/guidelines-and-manuals/actfl-proficiency-guidelines-2012
Asia Society (2014) *Expand World Language Programs*. See http://asiasociety.org/education/policy-initiatives/state-initiatives/expand-world-language-programs
Associated Press. (2010, December 8) Foreign language courses growing on campuses. *USA Today*. See http://usatoday30.usatoday.com/news/nation/2010-12-08-2010-12-08_N.htm
Bauer, D. and Mott, D. (1990) Life-themes and motivations of re-entry students. *Journal of Counseling and Development* 68, 555–60.
Beacco, J. (2011) The cultural and intercultural dimensions of language teaching: current practice and prospects. The Council of Europe. See http://www.coe.int/t/dg4/linguistic/EducInter_en.asp
Beglar, D. and Hunt, A. (2002) Implementing task-based language teaching. In J. Richards and W. Renandya (eds) *Methodology in Language Teaching: An Anthology of Current Practice* (pp. 96–106). Cambridge: University Press.
Benson, P. (2013) *Teaching and Researching: Autonomy in Language Learning*. New York: Routledge.
Bialystok, E. (1988) Levels of bilingualism and levels of linguistic awareness. *Developmental Psychology* 24 (4), 560–567.
Block, D. (2000) Revisiting the gap between SLA researchers and language teachers. *Links & Letters* 7, 129–43.
Borg, S. (2003) Teacher cognition in language teaching: A review of research on what language teachers think, know, believe, and do. *Language Teaching* 36 (2), 81–109.
Brady, A. (2006) University language study for civic education: A framework for students' participation to effect individual and social change. *Language Awareness* 15 (4), 229–43.
The British Council (2013) *Language Rich Europe: Multilingualism for Stable and Prosperous Societies*. See http://www.language-rich.eu/home/welcome.html
The British Council (2014) *Languages for the Future*. See http://www.britishcouncil.org/organisation/publications/languages-future
Brookfield, S. (1987) *Developing Critical Thinkers: Challenging Adults to Explore Alternative Ways of Thinking and Acting*. San Francisco: Jossey-Bass.
Brookfield, S. (1990) Analyzing the influence of media on learners' perspectives. In J. Mezirow (ed) *Fostering Critical Reflection in Adulthood* (pp. 177–193). San Francisco: Jossey-Bass.

Brookfield, S. (2005) *The Power of Critical Theory for Adult Learning and Teaching*. New York: Open University Press.
Brown, A. (2009) Students' and teachers' perceptions of effective foreign language teaching: A comparison of ideals. *The Modern Language Journal* 93 (1), 46–60.
Brown, C. (1985) Two windows on the classroom world: Diary studies and participant observation differences. In P. Larson, E.L. Judd and D.S. Messerschmitt (eds) *On TESOL '84: A Brave New World for TESOL* (pp. 121–134). Washington, D.C.: TESOL.
Brown, H. (2002) English language teaching in the 'Post-Method' Era: Toward better diagnosis, treatment, and assessment. In J. Richards and W. Renandya (eds) *Methodology in Language Teaching: An Anthology of Current Practice* (pp. 9–18). Cambridge: University Press.
Brown, H. (2007) *Principles of Foreign Language Learning and Teaching* (5th edn). NY: Pearson Education.
Buttaro, L. and King, K.P. (2001) Listening to our adult ESL learners: Hispanic women's seldom heard voices. *Adult Basic Education: An Interdisciplinary Journal for Adult Literacy Educators* 11 (1), 40–60.
Byram, M. (1997) *Teaching and Assessing Intercultural Communicative Competence*. Clevedon: Multilingual Matters.
Byram, M. (2008) *From Foreign Language Education to Education for Intercultural Citizenship: Essays and Reflections*. Clevedon: Multilingual Matters.
Byram, M. (2010) THE ISSUE Revisiting the role of culture in the foreign language curriculum. *Modern Language Journal* 94 (2), 315–7.
Byram, M., Gribkova, B., and Starkey, H. (2002) Developing the intercultural dimension in language teaching: A practical introduction for teachers. Strasborg: Council of Europe. See http://www.coe.int/t/dg4/linguistic/source/guide_dimintercult_en.pdf
Byram, K. and Kramsch, C. (2008) Why is it so difficult to teach language as culture? (Report). *The German Quarterly* 81 (1), 20.
Carlson, A. (1998) America's growing observance of *cinco de mayo*. *Journal of American Culture* 21 (2), 7–16.
Center for Applied Linguistics. (2010) Ñandutí. See http://www.cal.org/earlylang
Chambers, F. (1991) Promoting the target language use in the classroom. *Language Learning Journal* 4, 27–31.
Chau, L. (2014, January 29) Why you should learn another language: Those who speak more than one language have a greater chance of succeeding in business. *US News*. See http://www.usnews.com/opinion/blogs/economic-intelligence/2014/01/29/the-business-benefits-of-learning-a-foreign-language
Chaudron, C. (1988) *Second Language Classrooms: Research on Teaching and Learning*. Cambridge: University Press.
Chauvot, P. (2013, Dec 19) Why UK businesses need more language skills. *RealBusiness*. See http://realbusiness.co.uk/article/25079-why-uk-businesses-need-more-language-skills
Chávez, A.F., Guido-DiBrito, F., Mallory, S.L. (2003) Learning to value the 'Other': A framework of individual diversity development. *Journal of College Student Development* 44 (4), 453–69.
Citron, J. (2001) Can cross-cultural understanding aid second language acquisition? Toward a theory of ethno-lingual relativity. *Hispania* 78 (1), 105–113.
Clément, R. (1986) Second language proficiency and acculturation: An investigation of the effects of language status and individual characteristics. *Journal of Language and Social Psychoogy* 5 (4), 271–90

Coffey, A. and Atkinson, P. (1996) *Making Sense of Qualitative Data*. Thousand Oaks, CA: Sage Publications, Inc.
Cook, V. (2001) Using the first language in the classroom. *Canadian Modern Language Review* 57, 402–423.
Corral, W., and Patai, D. (2008, June 6) An end to foreign languages, an end to the liberal arts. [Electronic Version]. *The Chronicle of Higher Education* 54 (39). See http://chronicle.com/weekly/v54/i39/39a03001.htm
Council of Europe [COE]. (2014) Common European Framework of Reference for Languages: Learning, Teaching, Assessment. See http://www.coe.int/t/dg4/linguistic/Source/Framework_EN.pdf
Cranton, P. (2006) *Understanding and Promoting Transformative Learning: A Guide for Educators of Adults*. San Francisco: Jossey-Bass.
Creswell, J. (2007) *Qualitative Inquiry and Research Design: Choosing Among Five Approaches*. Thousand Oaks, CA: Sage Publications, Inc.
Cross, R. (2010) Language teaching as sociocultural activity: Rethinking Language teacher practice. *The Modern Language Journal* 94 (3), 434–452.
Davidson, J. (2012, May 21) Government has a language deficit. *Washington Post*. See http://www.washingtonpost.com/politics/government-has-foreign-language-deficit/2012/05/21/gIQAzjgVgU_story.html
Deardorff, D.K. (2006) Identification and assessment of intercultural competence as a student outcome of internationalization. *Journal of Studies in Intercultural Education* 10, 241–266.
Demont, E. (2001) Contribution of early 2nd-language learning to the development of linguistic awareness and learning to read/Contribution de l'apprentissage précoce d'une deuxième langue au développment de la conscience linguistique et à l'apprentissage de la lecture. *International Journal of Psychology* 36 (4), 274–285.
Denzin, N. (1970) *The Research Act*. Chicago: Aldine.
Dewey, J. (1938/1998) *Experience and Education*. Indianapolis, IN: Kappa Delta Pi.
Di Carlo, A. (1994) Comprehensible input through the practical application of video-texts in second language acquisition. *Italica* 71 (4), 465–83.
Dijkstra, W., Van der Veen, L. and Van der Zouwen, J. (1985) A field experiment on interviewer-respondent interaction. In M. Brenner, J. Brown, and D. Canter (eds) *The research interview: Uses and Approaches* (pp. 37–63). London: Academic Press.
Edstrom, A. (2006) L1 use in the L2 classroom: One teacher's self-evaluation. *The Canadian Modern Language Review* 63 (2), 275–292.
Elias, J. and Merriam, S. (2005) *Philosophical Foundations of Adult Education*. Malabar, Florida: Krieger Publishing Company.
Finney, D. (2002) The ELT curriculum: A flexible model for a changing world. In Richards, J. and W. Renandya (eds) *Methodology in Language Teaching: An Anthology of Current Practice* (69–79). Cambridge: University Press.
Foderaro, L. (2010, Dec 3) Budget-cutting colleges bid some languages adieu. *The New York Times*. See http://www.nytimes.com/2010/12/05/education/05languages.html?pagewanted=alland_r=0
Fortune, T.W. (2012) What the research says about immersion. In Asia Society. *Chinese Language Learning in the Early Grades: A Handbook of Resources and Best Practices for Language Immersion* (9–13). See http://asiasociety.org/files/chinese-earlylanguage.pdf
Foster, E. (1997) Transformative learning in adult second language learning. *New Directions for Adult and Continuing Education* 74, 33–40.
Foucault, M. (1972) *The Archeology of Knowledge*. New York: Pantheon.

Freire, P. (1970/2000) *Pedagogy of the Oppressed*. New York: The Continuum Publishing Corporation.
Fromkin, V., Rodman, R., and Hyams, N. (2003) *An Introduction to Language*. 7th (edn). Boston: Thompson Heinle.
Furman, N., Goldberg, D., and Lusin, N. (2007) Enrollments in languages other than english in united states institutions of higher education, Fall 2006. See http://www.mla.org/pdf/06enrollmentsurvey_final.pdf
Gallup Rodríguez, A. (2009) CAELA network briefs: Teaching grammar to adult english language learners: Focus on form. Center for Applied Linguistics. See http://www.cal.org/caelanetwork/resources/teachinggrammar.html
Gardner, R.C. (2001) Integrative motivation and second language acquisition. In Z. Dörnyei and R. Schmidt (eds) *Motivation and Second Language Acquisition* (Technical Report #23, 1–19). Honolulu: University of Hawai'i, Second Language Teaching and Curriculum Center.
Goulah, J. (2006) Transformative second and foreign language learning for the 21st century. *Critical Inquiry in Language Studies: An International Journal* 3 (4), 201–221.
Guy, T. C. (2007) Learning who we (and they) are: Popular culture as pedagogy. *New Directions for Adult and Continuing Education* 115, 15–23.
Hagood, J. (2013, December 5) Flipped Classroom: How to Create a Learning Community Outside of the Classroom. Presentation given at the Midwest Faculty Seminar – Preparing Future Faculty at the University of Chicago, Chicago, IL.
Hart, M. (1990) Liberation through consciousness raising. In J. Mezirow (ed) *Fostering Critical Reflection in Adulthood* (pp. 47–73). San Francisco: Jossey-Bass.
Holec, H. (1979) *Autonomy and Foreign Language Learning*. Strasbourg, France: Council for Cultural Cooperation.
Holliday, A. (2011) *Intercultural Communication and Ideology*. London: Sage Publications.
Hughes Wilhelm, K. (1997) Sometimes kicking and screaming: Language teachers-in-training react to a collaborative learning model. *The Modern Language Journal* 81 (4), 527–542.
Ingram, D.E. (2000) *Language Policy and Language Education in Australia*. See http://islpr.com.au/PDF/Language_Policy_Language_Education_Australia.pdf
Johnson, K. (2006) The sociocultural turn and its challenges for second language teacher education. *TESOL Quarterly* 40 (1), 235–257.
Johnson, S.M. and Mullins Nelson, B. (2010) Above and beyond the syllabus: Transformation in an adult, foreign language classroom. *Language Awareness* 19 (1), 35–50.
Kasworm, C. (2003) Setting the stage: Adults in higher education. *New Directions for Student Services* 102, 3–10.
Kegan, R. (1994) *In Over Our Heads: The Mental Demands of Modern Life*. Cambridge, MA: Harvard University Press.
Kennedy, W. (1990) Integrating personal and social ideologies. In J. Mezirow (ed) *Fostering Critical Reflection in Adulthood* (99–115). San Francisco: Jossey-Bass.
King, K. (2000) The adult ESL experience: Facilitating perspective transformation in the classroom. *Adult Basic Education: An Interdisciplinary Journal for Adult Literacy Educators* 10 (2), 69–89.
Kitchener, K. and King, P. (1990) The reflective judgment model: Transforming assumptions about knowing. In J. Mezirow (ed) *Fostering Critical Reflection in Adulthood* (159–176). San Francisco: Jossey-Bass.

Knowles, M., Holton, E., and Swanson, R. (2005) *The Adult Learner* (6th ed). Burlington, MA: Elsevier.

Knutson, E. (2006) Cross-cultural awareness for second/foreign language learners. *The Canadian Modern Language Review/La revue canadienne des langues vivantes* 62 (4), 591–610.

Kolb, D.A. (1984) *Experiential Learning: Experience as the Source of Learning and Development.* Englewood Cliffs, NJ: Prentice-Hall

Kozaki, Y, and Ross, S. (2011) Contextual dynamics in foreign language learning motivation. *Language Learning* 61 (4), 1328–1354.

Kramsch, C. (1993) Language study as border study: Experiencing difference. *European Journal of Education* 28 (3), 349–58.

Kubota, R. (2004) Critical multiculturalism and second language education. In B. Norton and K. Toohey (eds) *Critical Pedagogies and Language Learning.* Cambridge: University Press.

Kuhn, T. (1962) *The Structure of Scientific Revolutions.* Chicago: University of Chicago Press.

Kumaravadivelu, B. (2006) *Understanding Language Teaching: From Method to Postmethod.* Mahwah, NJ: Lawrence Erlbaum Associates.

Lane, B. (2013, Jul 30) Language vs. Football (Well, Rugby). *Inside Higher Ed.* See http://www.insidehighered.com/news/2013/07/30/debate-over-athletics-vs-academics-rages-after-australian-universitys-language-cuts

Lantolf, J., and Pohner, M. (2014) *Sociocultural Theory and the Pedagogical Imperative in L2 Education: Vygotskian Praxis and the Research/Practice Divide.* New York: Routledge.

Lee, G., and Janda, L. (2006) Successful multicultural campus: Free from prejudice toward minority professors. *Multicultural Education*, 14 (1), 27–30.

Levine, G.S. (2003) Student and instructor beliefs and attitudes about target language use, first language use, and anxiety: Report of a questionnaire study. *The Modern Language Journal* 87, 343–364.

Liddicoat, A. and Scarino, A. (2013) *Intercultural Language Teaching and Learning.* New York: Wiley-Blackwell

Lindberg, I. (2003) Second language awareness: What for and for whom? *Language Awareness* 12 (3/4), 157–171.

Lindeman, E. (1961) *The Meaning of Adult Education.* Montreal: Harvest House.

Lippi-Green, R. (1997) *English with An Accent: Language, Ideology, and Discrimination in the United States.* Psychology Press.

Mackey, A. and Gass, S. (2005) *Second Language Research: Methodology and Design.* Mahwah, New Jersey: Lawrence Erlbaum Associates.

Malone, M., Rifkin, B., Christian, D., and Johnson, D. (2005) Attaining high levels of proficiency: Challenges for foreign language education in the united states. See http://www.cal.org/resources/digest/attain.html

Marsick, V., and Watkins, K. (2001) Informal and incidental learning. *New Directions for Adult and Continuing Education* 89, 25–34.

McGraw-Hill. (2006) Dos Mundos (6th ed) Information center. See http://highered.mcgraw-hill.com/sites/0072959258/information_center_view0/new_to_the_sixth_edition.html

McKay, S. (2006) *Researching Second Language Classrooms.* Mahwah, New Jersey: Lawrence Erlbaum Associates, Inc.

McLean, C. A. (2007) Establishing credibility in the multicultural classroom: When the instructor speaks with an accent. *New directions for teaching and learning* 2007 (110), 15–24.

Metz, A. (1990) Why Sosúa? Trujillo's motives for Jewish refugee settlement in the Dominican Republic. *Contemporary Jewry* 11 (1), 3–28.
Mezirow, J. (1991) *Transformative Dimensions of Adult Learning*. San Francisco, CA: Jossey-Bass.
Mezirow, J. (1997) Transformative learning: Theory to practice. *New Directions for Adult and Continuing Education* 74, 5–12.
Mikayla Ortuño, M. (1991) Cross-cultural awareness in the foreign language class: The Kluckhohn model. *The Modern Language Journal* 75 (4), 449–59.
Mitchell, C. and Vidal, K. (2001) Weighing the ways of the flow: Twentieth century language instruction. *The Modern Language Journal* 85 (1), 26–38.
MLA [Modern Language Association]. (2007) *Foreign Languages and Higher Education: New Structures for a Changed World*. See http://www.mla.org/pdf/forlang_news_pdf.pdf
MLA (2011) *Call for Action on Federal Budget Cuts to Language and Humanities Programs*. See https://www.mla.org/ec_budget_cuts
MLA. (2012) *MLA Statement on Language Learning and United States National Policy*. See http://www.mla.org/ec_us_language_policy
MLA. (2014) Report of the MLA task force on doctoral study in modern language and literature. See http://www.mla.org/report_doctoral_study_2014
Moeller, A. and Nugent, K. (2014) Building intercultural competence in the language classroom. See the Central States Conference on the Teaching of Foreign Languages 2014 Report: Unlock the Gateway to Communication at http://www.csctfl.org/documents/2014Report/2014rpt.html
Moon, J. (2004) *A Handbook of Reflective and Experiential Learning: Theory and Practice*. RoutledgeFalmer.
National Center for Education Statistics. (2011) College navigator: Southwest tennessee community college. See http://nces.ed.gov/collegenavigator/?q=southwest+tennessee+community+college&s=all&id=221485
National Standards in Foreign Language Education Project (NSFLEP). (2015) World-readiness standards for learning languages (W-RSLL). Alexandria, VA: Author. See http://www.actfl.org/publications/all/world-readiness-standards-learning-languages.
National Virtual Translation Center. (2007) *Language learning difficulty for English speakers*. See http://www.nvtc.gov/lotw/months/november/learningExpectations.html retrieved January 2009).
Nguyen, H. and Kellogg, G. (2010) 'I had the stereotype that American were fat': Becoming a speaker of culture in a second language. *The Modern Language Journal* 94 (1), 56–73.
Norton, B. and Toohey, K. (2004) Critical pedagogies and language learning: An introduction. In B. Norton and K. Toohey (eds) *Critical Pedagogies and Language Learning* (pp. 1–17). Cambridge: University Press.
Norton, B. and McKinney, C. (2011) An identity approach to second language acquisition. In D. Atkinson (ed) *Alternative Approaches to Second Language Acquisition* (pp. 73–94). Routledge.
Norton, B. (2013) *Identity and Language Learning: Extending the Conversation*. Bristol: Multilingual Matters.
Nunan, D. (1992) *Research Methods in Language Learning*. Cambridge: University Press.
O'Malley, J. and Valdez Pierce, L. (1996) *Authentic Assessment for English Language Learners: Practical Approaches for Teachers*. New York: Addison-Wesley.
Osborn, T. (2006) *Teaching World Languages for Social Justice: A Sourcebook of Principles and Practices*. Mahwah, New Jersey: Lawrence Erlbaum Associates, Publishers.

Paesani, K. (2005) Literary texts and grammar instruction: Revisiting the inductive presentation. *Foreign Language Annals* 38 (1), 15–23.
Pearson Casanave, C. (2011) *Journal Writing in Second Language Education*. Ann Arbor: University of Michigan Press.
Pennycook, A. (2001) *Critical Applied Linguistics: A Critical Introduction*. Mahwah, New Jersey: Lawrence Erlbaum Associates, Publishers.
Peshkin, A. (1988) In search of subjectivity – One's own. *Educational Researcher* 17 (7), 17–22.
Pilling-Cormick, J. (1997) Transformative and self-directed learning in practice. *New Directions for Adult and Continuing Education* 74, 69–77.
Rachal, J. (2002) Andragogy's detectives: A critique of the present and a proposal for the future. *Adult Education Quarterly* 52 (3), 210–227.
Reagan, T. and Osborn, T. (2002) *The Foreign Language Educator in Society: Toward a Critical Pedagogy*. New York: Lawrence Erlbaum Associates.
Richards, J, and Rogers, T. (2001) *Approaches and Methods in Language Teaching*. Cambridge: University Press.
Rivers, W., Robinson, J., Harwood, P., and Brecht, R. (2013) Language votes: Attitudes toward foreign language policies. *Foreign Language Annals* 46 (3), 329–338.
Ross-Gordon, J. (2003) Adult learners in the classroom. *New Directions for Student Services* 102, 43–52.
Rossiter, M. (2007) Possible selves: An adult education perspective. *New Directions for Adult and Continuing Education* 114, 5–15.
Säljö, R. (1979) Learning about learning. *Higher Education* 8 (4), 443–451.
Schulz, R., and Elliott, P. (2000) Learning Spanish as an older adult. *Hispania* 83 (1), 107–19.
Schumann, J. (1986) Research on the acculturation model for second language acquisition. *Journal of Multilingual and Multicultural Development* 7 (5), 379–392.
Sheen, R. (2008) A critical analysis of the advocacy of the task-based syllabus. *TESOL Quarterly* 28 (1), 127–151.
Spradley, J. (1980) *Participant Observation*. New York: Holt, Rinehart & Winston.
Stauble, A. M. (1980) Acculturation and second language acquisition. In R. Scarcella and S. Krashen, S. (eds) *Research in Second Language Acquisition* (pp. 43–50).
Stoller, F. (2006) Establishing a theoretical foundation for project-based learning in second and foreign language contexts. In G.H. Beckett, and P.C. Miller (eds) *Project-Based Second and Foreign Language Education: Past, Present, and Future* (pp. 19–40). Greenwich, CT: Information Age Publishing.
Taylor, E.W. (1994) Intercultural competency: A transformative learning process. *Adult Education Quarterly* 44 (3), 154–174.
Taylor, E.W. (1997) Building upon the theoretical debate: A critical review of the empirical studies of Mezirow's transformative learning theory. *Adult Education Quarterly* 48 (1), 34–59.
Terrell, T., Andrade, M., Egasse, J. and Muñoz, E.M. (2005) *Dos Mundos* (6th edn). McGraw-Hill.
Tisdell, E. and Thompson, P. (2007) Seeing from a different angle: The role of pop culture in teaching for diversity and critical media literacy in adult education. *International Journal of Lifelong Education* 26 (6), 651–73.
Uber Grosse, C., Tuman, W., and Critz, M. (1998) The economic utility of foreign language study. *The Modern Language Journal* 82 (4), 457–472.

U.S. Census Bureau (2011) *2005–2009 American Community Survey 5-Year Estimates: Data Profile Highlights*. See http://www.census.gov/

U.S. Department of Education (2012) Foreign language assistance program. See http://www2.ed.gov/programs/flapsea/index.html

Ushioda, E., and Dörnyei, Z. (2012) Motivation. In S. Gass and A. Mackey (eds) *The Routledge handbook of second language acquisition* (pp. 396–409). New York: Routledge.

Whorf, B.L. (1956) *Language, Thought and Reality*. J.B. Carroll (ed) Cambridge, MA: MIT Press.

Wurdinger, S., and Carlson, J. (2010) *Teaching for Experiential Learning: Five Approaches That Work*. Lanham, MD: Rowman & Littlefield Education.

Zhou, C. (2013, Jun 21) Business calls for greater Asian language skills. *ABC News*. See http://www.abc.net.au/news/2013-06-21/business-calls-for-great-asian-language-skills/4772228

Zuengler, J. and Miller, E. (2006) Cognitive and sociocultural perspectives: Two parallel SLA worlds? *TESOL Quarterly* 40 (1), 35–58.

# Index

Abrams, Z. 30
Accent 51, 52, 67, 89–92, 115
ACTFL (American Council on the Teaching of Foreign Languages) 4, 28–29
Alexa (Participant) 48–49, 55, 64, 68, 81–2, 87, 91, 99–101, 104, 107, 109–110, 121
Alvarez, J. 69
Andrade, M. 57–58
Antonio (Participant), see Pérez
Anxiety 52, 62, 122
Asia Society 2, 3
Assessment,
 Learning/Learner 22, 55–56, 67, 102–104, 120, 124–126, 127–128
 Teaching/Teacher 126
 Critical 16, 21, 85, 93, 95, 104–106, 111
Atkinson, P. 8
Authority 54, 58
Autonomy 36, 54, 119, 125
Authentic 16, 31, 33, 37, 38, 70, 98, 118, 124
Awareness 25, 40, 45, 89, 106–107

Bauer, D. 52, 62
Beacco, J. 39
Beglar, D. 34
Bella (Participant) 49, 64, 68, 80, 83, 84–85, 87, 92, 93, 96, 97, 98, 102–3, 104, 105, 107, 109
Benson, P. 17
Bialystok, E. 20
Block, D. 29
Boovy, B. 30
Borg, S. 29, 59
Brady, A. 23
Brecht, R. 2
British Council 2
Brookfield, S. 24, 40–41, 70
Brown, A. 30, 117

Brown, C. 8
Brown, H. 30, 31, 32, 33, 34, 38, 39
Buttaro, L. 24
Byram, M. 4, 30, 39, 44, 45, 104, 125
Byrd, D. 30

Carlson, A. 105
Carlson, J. 10
Center for Applied Linguistics 2
Chao, Manu 82
Chau, L. 2
Chaudron, C. 8, 68
Chauvot, P. 2
Chávez, A.F. 25, 58, 74, 104, 106
Christian, D. 3
Citron, J. 24, 25, 44, 104
Clément, R. 44, 104
Coffey, A. 8
COE (Council of Europe) 4, 29, 45
Collaborative learning 23–24, 55, 63–65, 80, 111–112, 118–119, 123–124
Communicative competence/ability 3, 15, 24–25, 29, 31–32, 33–34, 35, 38, 45–46, 62, 82, 112, 122, 126, 127
Consciousness 4, 20–21, 23–24, 75, 125, 129
Cook, V. 122, 123
Corral, W. 34
Cranton, P. 23, 38, 67
Critical Reflection 21, 22, 23–24, 25–27, 30, 40–41, 56, 66, 67, 68, 70, 75, 78, 104–106, 110–111, 112, 120–123, 127–128
Critical pedagogy 40–41, 66, 71–72, 75, 120
Critz, M. 33,
Cross, R. 39, 40
Curriculum 5, 14, 29, 33, 35, 37–38, 57

Davidson, J. 2
Deardorff, D.K. 44, 45, 85

Degree Requirements 2, 3–4, 7, 48–51, 114, 128–129
Deep Learning 6, 7, 8, 10, 18, 23, 45, 48, 55–56, 77, 79, 92, 100, 109, 112, 114–115, 117, 121, 125, 128–129,
Demont, E. 20
Denzin, N. 9
Development
  Curriculum/Lesson 14, 117
  Diversity 26–27, 45, 74, 85, 104, 106, 115, 122, 123, 126, 128
  Language 25, 123
  Personal/Adult 5–6, 12–13, 17–18, 25, 29, 32, 100, 104, 114, 115, 116, 118, 120, 122, 123, 128
Dewey, J. 13, 14, 25, 37
Dina (Participant), see Salazar
Di Carlo, A. 30
Dijkstra, W. 9
Disorienting Dilemma 20–23, 55–56, 62, 64, 85, 95, 104, 107–111, 114, 117, 123, 127
Dörnyei, Z. 43
Dualistic 26, 42, 74, 106

Edstrom, A. 122
Egasse, J. 57–58
Elias, J. 12, 13, 32, 33, 34
Elliott, P. 62
Emily (Participant) 49, 58, 83, 84, 85, 91, 98, 99, 105, 108, 109, 110,
English, see L1 use
Ethnocentrism 19, 26
Ethnorelativity 25, 26, 104
Experience/Experiential Learning 13–16, 23, 37–38, 67, 117–120

Film 69–74, 75, 82, 87–88, 92, 101, 107, 111, 114, 122, 125
Finney, D. 36
Fluency 2–4, 13, 17, 31, 61, 93, 114, 122, 127, 129
Foderaro, L. 2
Fortune, T.W. 2
Foster, E. 24, 111
Foucault, M. 22
Freire, P. 24, 36, 40, 54–55, 66, 72, 78
Fromkin, V. 20
Furman, N. 128

Gallup Rodriguez, A. 32
Gardner, R.C. 24, 42, 102
Gass, S. 9
Goldberg, D. 128
Goulah, J. 24
Grammar/Vocabulary 4, 15–16, 18, 20, 32, 35, 37–38, 51–52, 57–58, 60–62, 65–66, 75, 77, 78–80, 83, 86, 112, 114, 117, 118, 122, 125, 127
Gribkova, B. 45
Group work, See collaborative learning
Guido-DiBrito, F. 25, 58, 74, 104, 106
Guy, T.C. 24, 30, 70, 75

Hagood, J. 5
Hart, M. 24
Harwood, P. 2
Holec, H. 17
Holliday, A. 45
Holton, E. 16, 17, 33, 34, 35, 36, 37, 56, 57, 94, 100
Hughes Wilhelm, K. 24
Hunt, A. 34
Hyams, N. 20

Identity 9, 19, 39, 41–44, 52, 101, 120
Incidental learning 38, 125
Ingram, D.E. 1
Integration 20–21, 26, 106
Interaction 29, 31, 61, 68, 82–83, 98, 112, 117, 120, 124, 130
Intercultural/transcultural competence 1, 3, 4, 13–14, 39, 44–46, 85, 98, 101, 104, 117, 119, 120–121, 122–123, 126, 128, 129
In the Time of the Butterflies, see Film
Investment 13, 39, 42–44, 56, 100–101, 115

Janda, L. 89
Jade (Participant) 9, 49–50, 65, 82, 86, 87–88, 93, 98, 99, 100, 101, 106, 107, 108, 109, 110, 111, 124
Joe (Participant) 50, 65, 86, 92–93, 97, 110
Johnson, D. 3
Johnson, K. 40, 129
Johnson, S. M. 7, 24, 25, 63, 92, 116, 117

Kasworm, C. 33, 94
Keisha (Participant) 50, 59–60, 64–65, 68, 81, 82, 84, 87, 90–91, 93, 104, 108, 110,
Kegan, R. 17–18, 25, 27, 100
Kellogg, G. 45
Kennedy, W. 19, 41
King, K. 22, 23, 24, 63, 110, 116, 117
King, P. 23
Kitchener, K. 23
Knowles, M. 16, 17, 33, 34, 35, 36, 37, 56, 57, 94, 100
Knutson, E. 23, 40, 58, 62, 66, 104
Kolb, D.A. 14–16, 37–38, 67, 118–119
Kozaki,Y. 43
Kramsch, C. 4, 30, 104, 125
Kubota, R. 45
Kuhn, T. 22
Kumaravadivelu, B. 30, 32, 35, 39, 126

L1 use 31, 33, 45–46, 52, 57, 60, 61–62, 63, 69, 75, 84, 97, 112, 120, 121–123, 125
Lane, B. 2
Lantolf, J. 29
Lee, G. 89
Levine, G.S. 122
Liberal arts 1, 11, 32–34, 61, 122–123
Liddicoat, A. 39
Lindberg, I. 62
Lindeman, E. 17, 25, 37, 97–98
Lippi-Green, R. 89
Lusin, N. 128

Mackey, A. 9
Mallory, S.L. 25, 58, 74, 104, 106
Malone, M. 3
Marsick, V. 38, 125
McGraw-Hill 57
McKay, S. 8
McKinney, C. 43
McLean, C.A. 89
Meaning making 14, 19, 40, 61, 63
Meaning perspectives 18–19, 20–23, 41, 42, 56, 75, 84, 112, 121–122, 123, 127
Merriam, S. 12, 13, 32, 33, 34
Metalinguistic awareness 20, 33, 62, 75, 84, 120

Metz, A. 73
Mezirow, J. 18, 19, 20, 21, 22, 23, 42, 55, 62, 72, 85, 95, 96, 100, 110, 112, 123
Mikayla Ortuño, M. 104
Miller, E. 39, 40
Mitchell, C. 31, 32
MLA (Modern Language Association) 2, 3, 4, 129
Moeller, A. 45
Mohring, A. 30
Moon, J. 14
Mott, D. 52, 62
Motivation 17, 24–25, 33–34, 39, 42–44, 56, 59, 100–104, 108, 115, 116
Mullins Nelson, B. 7, 24, 25, 63, 92, 116, 117
Muñoz, E.M. 57–58

National Center for Education Statistics 48
National Virtual Translation Center 3
Nguyen, H. 45
Norton, B. 41, 43, 75
Nugent, K. 45
Nunan, D. 68

O'Malley, J. 22
Osborn, T. 75

Paesani, K. 118
Patai, D. 34
Pearson Casanave, C. 67
Pedagogy
    Training for instructors 10–11, 129
    Critical 13, 39, 40–41, 45, 66, 71–72, 75, 120
Pennycook, A. 12, 24, 41, 42, 45
Pérez, Antonio (Participant) 51–52, 71, 72, 74, 75, 100
Perspective Transformation 20–22, 22–23, 23–24, 45, 58, 62, 72, 74, 82, 85, 95–113, 115–116, 129
Peshkin, A. 10
Pilling-Cormick, J. 24, 63
Pohner, M. 29
Project-based learning 17

Questioning 26–27, 45, 66, 75, 104, 106–107, 121, 123,

Rachal, J. 36
Reagan, T. 75
Richards, J. 29
Rifkin, B. 3
Rivers, W. 2
Robinson, J. 2
Rodman, R. 20
Rogers, T. 29
Ross, S. 43
Ross-Gordon, J. 36, 52, 54, 57, 62
Rossiter, M. 52

Salazar, Dina (Participant) 7–8, 49–51, 51–52, 53, 54, 58, 59–67, 67–69, 69–74, 75, 84–86, 89–91, 98, 100, 101, 103, 105, 125, 126
Säljö, R. 23, 78, 125
Sandy (Participant) 50–51, 80, 83, 84, 91, 96, 97, 110
Second Language Acquisition 12, 25, 29, 39, 40, 44, 79, 95
Self-Directed 5, 6, 13, 16–18, 36, 54, 57–58, 72–73, 95, 96, 100–104, 115, 121, 125
Scarino, A. 39
Schulz, R. 62
Schumann, J. 44
Sheen, R. 35
Socialization 19, 124
Sociocultural context 21, 39–46, 95
Spradley, J. 8,
Standards 4, 11, 28–29
Starkey, H. 45
Stauble, A.M. 44
Stoller, F. 17
Swanson, R. 16, 17, 33, 34, 35, 36, 37, 56, 57, 94, 100
Syllabus 10, 34–36, 56–58, 79, 125

Taylor, E.W. 45, 104, 115, 117
Ten (Participant) 9, 51, 55, 58, 65, 67, 68, 69, 86, 89, 90, 97, 98, 100, 103, 104, 106, 110,
Terrell, T. 57–58
Textbook 10, 35, 56–58, 60, 62, 63, 66, 97–98
Thompson, P. 24, 30
Tisdell, E. 24, 30
Toohey, K. 75
Transformative/Transformational Learning 1, 5, 6, 7, 13, 18–25, 30, 40, 41, 45, 56, 62, 64, 69, 77, 92, 95–113, 114–118, 120–124, 127
Tuman, W. 33

Uber Grosse, C. 33
US Census Bureau 47
US Department of Education, 2
Ushioda, E. 43

Van der Veen, L. 9
Van der Zouwen, J. 9
Valdez Pierce, L. 22
Values 19, 22, 23, 41, 43, 44, 62, 95, 118, 121, 125, 128
Vidal, K. 31, 32
Vocabulary, *see* Grammar/Vocabulary

Watkins, K. 38, 125
Whorf, B.L. 22
Wurdinger, S. 10

Zhou, C. 2
Zuengler, J. 39, 40

For Product Safety Concerns and Information please contact our EU Authorised Representative:

Easy Access System Europe

Mustamäe tee 50

10621 Tallinn

Estonia

gpsr.requests@easproject.com